Prayer:
REACHING
THE MOUNTAIN TOP

Prayer:
REACHING
THE MOUNTAIN TOP

A Practical Guide To Developing
A More Satisfying Prayer Life

LYNDA SCOTSON

To order additional copies of this book, contact:
Xlibris Corporation
0-800-644-6988
www.XlibrisPublishing.co.uk
Orders@XlibrisPublishing.co.uk
302046

CONTENTS

DEDICATION

This book is dedicated to all those secret prayers who change the world.
I wish to say a special word of thanks to my husband and sons for
graciously allowing me the time and space to complete this book.
Thank you too to all of those who have provided
encouragement and advice along the way.
Finally, but most importantly, thank you to the One who
continues to answer the request, 'Lord, teach me to pray'.

INTRODUCTION

PART ONE

Lead Me up the Mountain

$\mathcal{I}$t was sweleringly hot, a rare family day out during a holiday which was largely spent visiting my parents' elderly relatives. Our annual trip to Devon was the only opportunity Mum and Dad had to see their own family, and they wanted to make the most of it.

So here we were in Dartmoor, myself and my brother, our parents, my mother's twin sister, and her family—four adults, three boys, and me, a naturally solitary child made more so by age and gender.

As the adults talked and the boys splashed around in the boulder-strewn stream, I decided to make for the top of the hill and take in the panoramic view I would be able to enjoy of unspoiled moorland, brilliant yellow gorse, and impossibly wide skies.

It didn't take me long to discover this was not going to be the short and simple jaunt I had imagined. I set my sights at the top of the hill and began to climb. In just a few moments, I had reached my goal, but instead of the expected sense of awe for the majesty of creation laid out before me, what I saw was another peak which had been hidden by the undulations of the hill. I was going to have to climb further.

This expectation and disappointment was repeated four or five times. I could no longer see my family at the water's edge. My world became simply the tor, the apparently never-ending rocky outcrop of wilderness. I decided to make one more climb towards the next peak, now lacking the original confidence and enthusiasm of the first part of the trek.

I arrived at yet another grassy, rocky knoll with nothing more exciting to see than rabbit droppings. Now I was feeling unsettled, not only out of sight but also out of earshot of my family some distance below. I gave up and went back down to the foot of the tor, never seeing the glory of Dartmoor stretched out before me.

Our prayer lives can be like my abortive trek up that Dartmoor tor. We start out as new Christians, thrilled with our daily times of prayer and delighting in our new relationship with God. But over time, our joy diminishes because the Lord wants us to move on, to climb higher.

The question is, how do we do this? In almost everything else in life, we are provided with educators. As children, we have parents and schoolteachers to train our bodies and minds. Many employers provide work-based training. In our spiritual lives, we have pastors and preachers to expound God's Word to us and teach us how to live the Christian life. Today if you don't have a person to teach you about something, then there are numerous books and the Internet. It isn't even true any more that babies don't come with instruction manuals for the parents. Walk into any newsagent, and you will find several different magazines for new or aspiring parents.

But when it comes to prayer, there is nothing. That is not to say there are no books on prayer. A quick search on Amazon reveals over 25,000 books in the •category of *Christian Worship and Devotion*. But where is the book or where is the teacher, who will actually take us by the hand and lead us up the mountain? Where are the spiritual sherpa who will teach us to pray?

The problem is that, whilst we may be taught the first baby steps in prayer, there seems to be very few Christians in our generation who have themselves gone beyond these steps. Many years ago, I read the result of a survey conducted by a popular Christian magazine. I was so shocked by it that I have never forgotten it—the average church leader was typically spending ten minutes each day in prayer. Now God is not a clock-watcher when it comes to our prayer times, but I'm pretty sure no minister could be praying consistently for his congregation and seeking vision for his church in ten minutes a day, let alone have his own spiritual needs met.

It is not surprising then that many of us have not ventured beyond the type of prayer epitomised by the mnemonic ACTS—adoration, confession, thanksgiving, supplication. It's a great way to begin to pray, but it is limited because, for one thing, it leaves no room for listening, and God has always intended that communication with his people should be mutual.

The other favourite guide for prayer is what we have come to call The Lord's Prayer. It is a model prayer, given by the Lord Jesus, in response to his disciples' heartfelt request to teach them how to pray. Interestingly, it does not comply with the ACTS system. For those who firmly believe that confession must come before supplication, it is a challenge because in The Lord's Prayer we are taught to ask for our daily needs to be met before we ask for our sins to be forgiven.

Study of this prayer certainly has value in learning about prayer, but there are already many books which take that approach. What I want to draw your attention to, as we begin our journey into prayer together, is that The Lord's Prayer is in fact the answer to a prayer. Like the first disciples, we can and should ask the Lord, 'Teach me how to pray'. As we come humbly, recognising our inability to do this on our own, he will indeed teach us and lead us into previously undiscovered regions of prayer.

PART TWO

How to Use this Book

Reading a book on prayer is rather like reading a book on training to climb a mountain. It may be very interesting, but it's rather pointless unless you do something with it. My goal is to give you material you can try out, put into practice, and so transform your prayer life.

To that end, I have included 'exercises' for you to have a go at. Some of them may be very simple, while some will seem quite challenging. But they are each aimed at taking you a little further up the mountain. They have all been part of my own prayer journey at some point. So please don't skip over them and simply move on to the next bit of the book, but complete the exercise before you continue. It may be that you don't find every exercise helpful, but you won't know until you try, and you may be quite surprised by what is beneficial to you.

Try not to rush through the book too eagerly. It's probably best not to tackle more than one chapter at a time. The book has been designed to lead you step by step, so dashing on ahead could mean you miss some of the benefits along the way. A slow but steady approach is best, perhaps taking a chapter a day.

One of the things that I have discovered, as I've listened to people's comments after I've preached on prayer, is that they don't quite know how to worship in their personal times alone with the Lord. For many people, worship has become synonymous with corporate singing. But I have found that worship and adoration (the difference between the two will become clear later in the book) are absolutely key to a healthy prayer life. So I've included a section of *Devotions*, which may be used at any time either on their own or as part of your personal prayer times. I hope you will use them, but most of all, I hope they will be stepping stones towards your own personal expressions of worship and adoration of God.

The next thing I want to say is, please, please look up the Bible references and read them. They are the most important part of this book. God loves to speak to us through his Word. It may be that he has something for you other than what I have drawn from any particular passage.

Finally, do get a notebook to write things in. Some of the exercises will require you to write, but you will also want to keep track of how God is speaking to you as you endeavour to grow your prayer life.

I pray that you will grow in love for our Father and the Lord Jesus as you work through this book.

A Word of Warning

In our experience-driven generation, some Christians have fallen into the trap of using prayer and worship to try to find emotional highs, physical 'manifestations', or encounters with supernatural beings. There is no doubt that through prayer God does sometimes give extraordinary supernatural blessings. But we should never seek these. We should only ever seek the face of God. To elevate a desire for visions, encounters with angels, or even an experience of the profound depth of the love of God above the desire to worship him, simply because he is worthy of our worship, is nothing short of idolatry. We are always to seek the Giver, not the gift. Then if we are graced with such gifts, we will not become full of pride, thinking ourselves somehow better than those who have not been blessed in such a way; neither will we want to boast of our experiences, for they will be sacred to us, something which has grown out of the uniquely intimate relationship we share with our Lord.

Be wary of those who talk about remarkable supernatural experiences. Don't be overawed by such people and their claims. Don't envy them their experience. You are uniquely special to our heavenly Father. You are an individual, a one-off; there is no one else in the world who can offer prayer and worship to God in the way you can. He wants *your* worship, not a poor copy of someone else's worship. He has gifts for you in your prayer journey which are uniquely suited to you for the stage you are at. Entrust yourself to him, diligently seek only him, and you will find that he graces you with your own mountaintop experience, for he is the rewarder of all those who do indeed seek diligently (Heb. 11:6).

REACHING THE MOUNTAIN TOP

CHAPTER 1

On the Mountain of the Lord

On the mountain of the Lord it will be provided.

(Genesis 22:14)

The mountain peaks, the psalmist says (Ps. 95:4), belong to God. Many of the most significant occasions in scripture have occurred on mountaintops: the salvation of mankind when the ark came to rest on the mountains of Ararat; the laws given to Moses on Sinai; Elijah's sacrifice being consumed by fire before the prophets of Baal on Carmel; Solomon building the first temple on Mount Moriah. So mountains have become symbolic of encounters with God.

It is common in Christian parlance to use the phrase *mountaintop experience* to describe rare but special moments of closeness to God. The idea comes from the Gospel account of the Transfiguration of Jesus on the mountain where his glory was revealed to the disciples and overwhelmed them. They wanted to stay there. We too would like to stay on the mountaintop.

Abraham's experience on Mount Moriah was completely different. He was to go up the mountain to sacrifice his son, the son of promise, Isaac, through whom he had the promise of being the father of a great nation. Even so, Abraham had his own mountaintop experience, his own life-transforming encounter with God.

If we examine these two accounts (Gen. 22:1-19, Matt. 17:1-9), we find common themes which help to give us some insight into our own journey up the mountain to meet God in prayer.

Recognise the Call

The first thing to notice is that there is a call to go up the mountain. To Abraham, God said, 'Go.' Peter, James, and John were led by Jesus. Repeatedly he says to his disciples, 'Come. Come follow me, come to me all you who are weary, whenever two or more come together there I am.' Abraham and the disciples came to the Lord by climbing a mountain; we come to him in prayer. We are told to pray continually (1 Thess. 5:8), pray in the Spirit on all occasions (Eph. 6:18), be faithful in prayer (Rom. 12:12), and to devote ourselves to prayer (Col. 4:2). There is not a single disciple who is not called by God to a life of prayer, to a daily journey into the mountains.

Go!

It is not enough to recognise the call. I've heard so many people claim to know they should pray but admit to the fact that they either struggle to do so or have simply given up. What if Abraham had not gone to Moriah? Who would have blamed him for saying 'no', knowing what it could cost him? What if the three had not allowed Jesus to lead them up the mountain? What if I don't pray? No, the call is there, and God expects us to respond. The trick the devil plays on us is to get us to focus on what seems to be the onerous task of climbing the mountain, rather than the joy that awaits us at the top. Jesus is our example. For the joy set before him, he endured the cross (Heb. 12:2). We too may find that the prayer life has its difficult moments. But there is joy to be had and deeply intimate times with God for those who will persist because 'on the mountain of the Lord it will be provided'. If you are seeking real joy, genuine peace, and a love beyond knowing, the only place you will find it is through prayer.

Nancy Missler, in her book, *Private Worship: The Key To Joy*, explains that the root of the word *joy* is the same as that of *join*. Joy comes from unity, and the greatest joy comes from joining ourselves with God through prayer and worship.

Make the Effort

Mountain climbing, even hill walking, is not a stroll in the park. Many people don't go beyond the basics of prayer because they don't want to make the effort. The journey up the mountain is going to require discipline and self-sacrifice from the beginning. You need help. Very rarely will God call an individual to a deeper prayer life without providing some support at the beginning. Abraham had servants with him for the first part of the journey. The disciples had Jesus himself, and we can rely on his direct leading and the people and resources he places in our path. The business of prayer is not just praying but reading the Bible and other books that teach on prayer. We are treading an unfamiliar path, and we need a guide and an awareness of possible pitfalls.

Separate Yourself

Abraham reached the point where he had to leave his servants and go on alone with Isaac. Communal prayer is a vital part of our Christian life, but solitary prayer, the believer alone with the Lord, is even more so. You cannot transact serious personal business with God when there are other people around. Look at the Lord Jesus and see how many times in the Gospels it is recorded that he went to a solitary place, or to the wilderness, or even up a mountain to pray. In the Garden of Gethsemane, he wanted his disciples close at hand to pray for him, but it wasn't a prayer meeting. He went a little way away from them to deal with God alone. We too have to separate ourselves for prayer. If we don't, we'll just be milling around with the crowd at the foot of the mountain, missing out on an encounter of deep intimacy with God.

As has been said before, the prayer life is a love affair with 'Love Himself'. Anyone who's been in love knows they want to spend time alone with their beloved and that there are things which happen in private which are not appropriate to be shared with the wider world. The same is true of prayer and will become more so as the relationship develops.

Prepare Yourself for Worship

Abraham took wood, fire, and a knife with him. He went prepared for worship, and when he reached the place for the sacrifice, he built an altar. Preparation for worship is not often talked about, perhaps because of the emphasis on our right as redeemed people to enter God's presence with boldness. As human beings, we have a tendency to drift either towards legalism or towards license, and it is appropriate to reflect on how we worship and redress the balance if necessary. We must not be in such fear of the Lord that we are unable to face the thought of entering his presence. Equally, we must not become so casual that our liberty deteriorates into irreverence.

It troubles me that believers watch television on a Sunday morning before going to church or listen to a secular radio station as they drive to the worship meeting. Many services seem 'dead' simply because people come to them without having prepared themselves to meet with God and so they are not ready, let alone eager, to worship. The Jews, as they went up to Jerusalem for the great feasts, would prepare themselves with Psalms. Psalms 121 to 134 are known as the *Songs of Ascent*. Worshippers used them to 'tune in' to God *before* they reached the Temple.

Whether we come to corporate or personal worship, we need to prepare. Just as Abraham did, we need to ensure that we have with us all we need. In practical, terms that may mean a Bible, a hymn book, a notepad; in terms of place, it may mean a room, a chair, a CD player, and in terms of personal preparation, it may mean a time of silence, relaxation exercises, breathing techniques. All of these will be discussed in more detail later. For now, we simply need to acknowledge that preparation is vital to worship.

Have Faith God Will Meet with You

There was no doubt in Abraham's mind, God would be involved—he would be there; he would provide the lamb.

God created us with one purpose in mind, and that is to enjoy our company. Before the Fall, he walked with Adam in Eden. All of creation had been declared 'good', but only after man was created did God call what he had made 'very good'. When mankind rebelled, God's first response was to call out, 'Where are you?' The whole of history from that point on has been about finding a way to restore lost fellowship. That has been accomplished at the Cross, the veil has been torn in two, and we have access to God (Heb. 10:19-22). He himself has opened up the way. So, we can have confidence that he wants to meet with us. Contrary to what many of us have been taught in our churches, it really doesn't matter what state we are in when we come to him as long as our heart is set on seeking him. If we are riddled with sin but truly seeking the face of Jesus, his Holy Spirit will show us our faults and lead us to repentance. If we come in grief and despair, the Comforter will wrap us in his arms and love us. If we come with joy, he will rejoice with us. However we come, he will meet us.

Now, I can hear protests from people saying, 'Yes, but what about those times when I pray and the words seem to bounce back off the ceiling without ever getting anywhere near heaven?' Let me gently suggest that you are looking in the wrong direction. As a Christian, you are a temple of the Holy Spirit. God himself is living in you, closer to you than your own breath. Of course, he hears your prayers. They come to him as incense presented in golden bowls (Rev. 5:8). Your prayers are infinitely precious to him. The feeling that your prayers are going nowhere is simply that—a feeling. And feelings are not to be trusted. They can be affected by emotions, relationships, changing circumstances, and even the weather. No, regardless of how you feel about your prayers, you can be confident that God hears the words and feels the heart from which they come. Of course, that is not the same as saying that God answers all our prayers with a resounding 'yes!' That is a different matter altogether. But we certainly can have the faith that God will hear and meet us in prayer.

Offer a Sacrifice of Worship

Abraham went up the mountain with one purpose in mind, to make a sacrifice to God. In the biblical mindset, sacrifice and worship were inseparable. Appearing before God empty-handed was unthinkable (Ex. 23:15). Everyone brought some kind of offering—if it wasn't a bull, it was a lamb, if not a lamb then a dove or grain, wine, oil, money. Whatever was brought had to be the best and had to cost the owner something. David, for example, refused to make a sacrifice of something that was offered to him as a gift (2 Sam. 24:18-25).

Now, we know that we do not need to make sacrifice for our sins because Jesus became the once-for-all sacrifice for us (Heb. 9:24-28). But that is not the only reason for sacrifice. The Jews were also instructed about tithes and fellowship offerings. Jesus himself spoke highly of the sacrifice of the poor widow who, although offering very little in monetary value, actually made an enormous sacrifice (Luke 21:1-4). It wasn't simply 'all she had to live on' for that day, but for the foreseeable future. She probably had no idea when she would next hold money in her hands; she wasn't going to receive a regular pension payment every Thursday. The woman who broke the alabaster jar of perfume over Jesus (Luke 7:36-38) wasn't just giving away her most precious material possession but her hope of marriage too as it would have been her dowry.

But how many of us come to worship with the intention of offering sacrifice? In our materialistic culture, we more often come to receive than to give. We want to enjoy the worship, we want to hear teaching that encourages us, we want to feel the presence of God. If we don't get what we want, then we're off to find another church where the style of worship suits our particular taste or where the preacher has a reputation for expounding scripture in a way which concurs with our expectations of the kind of God we want to know.

This kind of experience hunting is not restricted to the charismatic element of the church, though perhaps it is more identifiable there. But no one wants to come home from the Sunday morning service feeling that it's cost them something to be there, and everyone would like their personal devotions to leave them feeling uplifted and refreshed. Sacrifice is not something we want to engage with.

Yet our personal experience tells us that when we love someone, we want to give to them, and the more we love, the more we want to give, even if it costs us a great deal. We have all heard examples of people risking death to save others or giving up their own lives to care for sick or dying loved ones. So why, when sacrifice is recognised as heroic, do we take a completely different view in our relationship with God? Look at the way we live. The average person spends thirty hours a week devoted to the one-eyed god in the corner of the living room though such is our devotion that it's now found its way into many bedrooms and kitchens too. Let's suppose the typical Christian is so busy with church activities that they spend only half that time in front of the TV—that's still almost a tithe of our time. What would happen if we sacrificed our favourite soap operas and tithed our time to God? What do you think he could do with us if we loved him enough to sacrifice just two and a half hours a day to prayer, worship, and Bible reading? Then there's the time we spend in our cars. Many people spend five or more hours a week on their daily commute to work. What if, instead of putting the secular music station on, worship or teaching CDs were feeding our minds and spirits? Could it be that your problem of anger with other drivers has more to do with what you're listening to than their incompetence?

But sacrifice is about much more than how we use our time. It's about deciding we're still going to worship in the midst of trouble—the Lord gives, the Lord takes away, blessed be the name of the Lord (Job 1:21). It's about praying for your enemies. It's about forgiving the betrayal by a friend who's completely misunderstood and misjudged you. It's about having your devotions in the bathroom at 5:30 a.m. because that's the only time and place you can be alone. It's about confessing to a trusted mentor those unmentionable sins that you'd rather not admit even to yourself, just so you know you will be held to account the next time the temptation comes. Sometimes it's simply about continuing to breathe when you'd rather die. And sometimes it's just trusting God when nothing makes sense, believing against the evidence of your own eyes and despite feeling as though he's deserted you.

Worship means very little without sacrifice. Anyone can recite words of worship just as anyone can recite words of love. The evidence of whether we really mean it is whether we are still saying those words in the tough times.

Expect God to Speak

In my youth, I was a member of a church drama group called *Grassroots*. One of the sketches in our repertoire was based on the Lord's Prayer. The only character on stage was kneeling at a chair, hands folded, eyes closed. She began, 'Our Father which art in heaven,' at which point a deep, disembodied male voice was heard, 'Yes?' And so the prayer pressed on, trying to complete her ritual while God struggled to get a word in edgeways.

Most of us, like the character in that sketch, don't honestly expect God to speak. If we do accept that others hear God's voice (whatever that may mean), we certainly don't expect that he will have something he wants to say to us. The problem is that there is an element of self-fulfilling prophecy here. We don't expect God to speak, so we're not listening for that still small voice which whispers into our hearts. Or we expect that he will only speak in certain ways or at certain times, and so our ability to hear what he is saying is limited. We will talk more about learning how to listen to God later. For now, I want to assure you that God is in the business of a two-way conversation and that he always has something to say.

The number one thing that God says to us in every way imaginable is, 'I love you.' God is love (1 John 4:16). This message is so important. It is not simply that God is loving—if that were the limit, then he could choose not to love certain people or refrain from loving us when we do something wrong. No, what John says in his first epistle is that this God we worship is love. This love (the original Greek language of the New Testament has four different words for love) is *agape* love, a kind of selfless love which is only perfectly expressed by God. This love is shown in many ways but most vehemently in the cross of Christ—for God so loved the world that he gave his one and only Son that whoever believes in him shall not perish but have eternal life (John 3:16). The cross stands at the centre of history, proclaiming the love of God for every single member of humanity throughout all ages. You and I are both people included in that all-embracing word, 'whoever,' and so, to you and me God is saying in words that echo through-out time and eternity, 'I love you.' Since God is continually saying those words to you, it is unthinkable that he would not have other things to say, guidance to offer, wisdom to impart, words of correction and discipline. Of course, he wants to speak to you. Come with an open mind and open heart expecting him to speak, and you will learn the sound of his voice (John 10:27).

Expect God to Provide

We are told that one of the outcomes of Abraham's experience on the mountain was that people began to say, 'On the mountain of the Lord it will be provided' (Gen. 22:14). In his case, it was the lamb for the sacrifice. From our perspective, there are two main ways in which we can see God providing for us through prayer.

The first is that he answers our prayers of petition. We ask for something—our daily bread, healing for a relative, salvation for a friend—and God answers. We will deal more with this later on when we consider how to pray according to God's will. For now, I simply want to encourage you to pray for those things you need with the expectation that our Father longs to give good gifts to his children (Matt. 7:11).

The second way in which God provides is more fundamental, and again it is something we will need to look at in more depth later. In fact, it is the basis for the entire business of living a *successful* Christian life and it is this. Jesus said, 'Apart from me you can do nothing' (John 15:5). Nothing is a very big word. We often read these big words of Jesus and gloss over them, but Jesus only ever said what he meant. What he meant on this occasion was that we need him to enable us to do everything we are required to do in order to bear fruit for him. It is true of the whole of our walk with him, and it is especially true of prayer. I firmly believe that the main reason why we struggle with motivation to pray, finding time to pray, getting answers to prayer, and so on is because we try to do it in our own strength. We think we need to work up the desire within us to pray, we think we should figure out what to pray, we think we have to pray for every need we become aware of. No, going down that route is a recipe for disappointment and failure. We need to understand that the only way to learn to pray is to entrust ourselves to our personal prayer tutor and expert in the matter, the Lord Jesus Christ. We cannot do it on our own. We must do as the disciples did and ask, 'Lord, teach us to pray' (Luke 11:1). We can do that with the confident expectation that he will provide all we need to enable us to pray.

Expect Jesus to Touch You Tenderly

Some people are afraid of prayer because they are afraid of God. They know God is holy, righteous, and perfect. They know they are deeply sinful and that the Lord disciplines those he loves. They become fearful of entering his presence because they expect to be told off and punished. Or they expect God is going to require a sacrifice of Abrahamic proportions and ask them to give up something they dearly want to hold on to. But this is a complete misrepresentation of how God deals with his people.

We have already talked about the love of God. This love did not require Abraham to slaughter his son but instead provided a ram. On the mount of transfiguration, when the disciples fell to the ground in terror, Jesus made a point of comforting them with his touch. Yes, our God is awesome, but he deals with us tenderly. When he shows us our sin, he does so in such a gentle way that we long to flee from it and run to him for cleansing and forgiveness. If he asks something of us, it is with such grace that we trust him to only do what is best for us.

He is also the great Healer who will touch our wounded soul with so much compassion that our places of deepest hurt become sacred. All of us are wounded by this sin-ridden world. We have been 'abused', neglected, rejected; we have experienced loss of loved ones, self-esteem, personal health. We have become withdrawn, angry, frighteningly weak. Most of the time, we hide these painful wounds away, clutching them close to ourselves for fear that someone will touch that sore spot and cause us to jump with pain. Everyone's pain is different, even the same kinds of events are experienced differently by different individuals. No one can possibly know what it is like to be you, to have suffered the way you have. No one has walked in your shoes, except Jesus. He has been with you every step of the way, and because he lives in you by his Holy Spirit, he genuinely does know exactly how you feel, and he understands you better than you do yourself. His compassion is boundless and, as you allow him into those deep recesses where you hide your pain, he will bring his tender touch, his healing hand, and his promised peace (John 14:27).

There is undoubtedly some value in sharing our pain with a trusted friend, counsellor, or confessor, but ultimately it is the Lord Jesus who transforms us from the inside out. It is in the place of prayer where we are healed and made whole.

Keep the Secrets

All intimate relationships have secrets which are not spoken about beyond the confines of the relationship. It is the case with close friends and with families—it is also the case in our relationship with God. It is true that Abraham's experience has been given to us for our benefit, but Jesus said to the disciples as they came down from the mountain, 'Don't tell anyone what you have seen until the Son of Man has been raised from the dead.' Paul spoke of experiences of the third heaven which he was not permitted to talk about (2 Cor. 12:4), Daniel had a revelation which was not to be given to God's people straight away (Dan. 12:4), and we know very little of what passed between the Lord Jesus and the Father during most of his times of prayer. God has things he wants to tell us and show us which he wants us to keep to ourselves. It may be a personal revelation of his love or his glory; it may be some encouragement or opening up of his plan for the future. It may be words of discipline, it may be something which makes no sense at the time and only becomes clear later on. But one thing we can be sure of, God will stop sharing his secrets if you keep showing them off to others. The quickest way to put a damper on your ability to hear from God is to fail to keep his confidence.

That is not to say you should never share anything about your private times with the Lord with anyone else. But you do need to learn to be discerning about what it is appropriate to share and what should remain closeted in your heart. This is probably one of those lessons that can only be learnt by trial and error. To begin with, you may not know what to keep secret; you may be so overjoyed by your encounter with the Lord that you want to share it with everyone, and you don't understand why you shouldn't. But then the next time you shut yourself away with him, you've lost the sense of his intimate presence. Everything seems dry—He is waiting for you to apologise for not keeping his secret before he will reveal himself to you again. If you are attentive, you will learn very quickly what needs to be kept between you and your Lord, but a simple rule of thumb about sharing your experiences is *if in doubt, don't.* You will also discover that the things you keep secret become more precious to you for not having been told.

Go Back Down the Mountain

Prayer can become addictive. There is a phase on this journey when, like the disciples, you begin to experience some of the glory of God, and his presence becomes so wonderful and so real that you genuinely don't want to leave. You want to stay on that mountaintop, worshipping God forever. Instead of how it used to be, finding 'urgent' things to do which require your attention before you settle to prayer and perpetually putting off your quiet time with the Lord, daily life becomes an irritation, an unwanted intrusion into time you want to give to prayer. Like newly-weds on honeymoon, you only have eyes for Jesus, and you are preoccupied with the process of learning intimacy.

Critics may say of believers at this stage of their spiritual development that they are, 'too heavenly minded to be any earthly good'. That simply betrays a lack of understanding about the growth of the prayer life and says more about the maturity of the speaker than of the person they are criticising. This time of prolonged mountaintop experience is important, but it is not the end of the journey. We must be careful that we take note of where Jesus is and follow him. The mountaintop is one of the places Jesus takes us because of a particular work he wants to accomplish in our lives. He will keep us there, delight us with his felt presence, cause us to long after him to the exclusion of all else. But there will come a time when he knows we need to go back down the mountain.

Probably every disciple who's ever been on that mountaintop experiences some level of distress when the Lord starts to lead them away from there. They think they have found heaven on earth, and they fear that they are losing something of their intimacy with Jesus. What they don't seem to understand is that leaving the mountaintop does not mean leaving Jesus because he comes back down the mountain with us.

It is only right that, since the focus of this book is on getting up the mountain, we should be clear from the outset that this is just the beginning of a life journey into prayer, and however far we go along the road, there is always more to be learnt.

Exercise

Ask the Lord to take you on your own personal journey towards the mountain peak. Examine your heart and make some written notes about both the things that excite you about this journey and the things which make you anxious about it. Take some time to offer each of these to Jesus, asking him to help you trust him with each one. As you progress, you will be able to look back and see how the Lord has honoured your commitment.

CHAPTER 2

Intimacy with God

Why is it so important that you are with God and God alone on the mountaintop? It's important because it's the place in which you can listen to the voice of the One who calls you the beloved. To pray is to listen to the One who calls you 'my beloved daughter,' 'my beloved son,' 'my beloved child.' To pray is to let that voice speak to the centre of your being, to your guts, and let that voice resound in your whole being.

(Henri Nouwen)

It seems to me that there are three kinds of prayers: those who don't, except in emergencies, those who do, but only out of duty, and those who love to pray because they have discovered that it is the doorway to intimacy with God.

When the Holy Spirit plants in our heart the seed of a desire for greater intimacy with God, the only thing that can satisfy our soul is to experience the love of Jesus in a deeply personal way. As St Isaac the Syrian is quoted as saying in *Listening to God* by Joyce Huggett,

Thirst after Jesus and He will satisfy you with His love.

It is clear from Paul's prayer in Ephesians 3:14-21 that this was his desire for the Ephesian believers:

> *For this reason I kneel before the Father, from whom his whole family in heaven and on earth derives its name. I pray that out of his glorious riches he may strengthen you with power through his Spirit in your inner being, so that Christ may dwell in your hearts through faith. And I pray that you, being rooted and established in love, may have power, together with all the saints, to grasp how wide and long and high and deep is the love of Christ, and to know this love that surpasses knowledge—that you may be filled to the measure of all the fullness of God. Now to him who is able to do immeasurably more than all we ask or imagine, according to his power that is at work within us, to him be glory in the church and in Christ Jesus throughout all generations, for ever and ever! Amen.*

Throughout scripture, both in the Old and New Testaments, the relationship between God and his people is described in terms of a marriage. The word *bride* is frequently used as, sadly, *adulteress* when there is a turning away from the Lord to foreign gods. In Paul's teaching on marriage in Ephesians 5:22-33, he makes it clear that marriage, including in the *one flesh* aspect of the relationship, is designed as an illustration of Christ's spiritual relationship with his Church. As Paul says, this is a profound mystery.

Many of us as evangelicals are uncomfortable talking about personal prayer in these terms. Perhaps the language sounds too close to that used in Catholic mysticism or monastic spirituality. But then we are faced with Solomon's Song of Songs. What is this account of passion doing in our Bibles? I have been told it is there to show us that physical intimacy between a husband and wife is a God-given gift to be enjoyed. If that is the sole reason for its inclusion, then we evangelicals have an even bigger problem because the wedding doesn't occur until the end of chapter 3, and there is much lovemaking before that! The primary reason for the inclusion of the Song in scripture is that it is, like the relationship it portrays, an illustration of the depth of spiritual communion possible between the believer and their Lord.

Is it too indulgent for a Christian to take time simply to develop their love relationship with the Lord? Shouldn't prayer be for intercession on behalf of others? Wouldn't an hour that has been given to basking in the love of Jesus be better spent performing some act of service?

Recently as I was preparing to speak to a small group of believers, I had an interesting experience. As I sought the Lord for his Word to those people, he asked me a rather probing question, 'If this were to be the last sermon you had the chance to preach, what would you want to say?' I thought about Paul.

Most of us do not know the day or hour of our departure from this world to the next, but it appears that the Apostle Paul believed he knew when his life would come to an end, and he set about writing some of the most moving passages of scripture. The letters to the Ephesians, Philippians, and Colossians are full of the heart of a man who wants believers to understand what really matters in the Christian life. Through these epistles, he preached what he considered his final words to the church.

Interestingly, the great Apostle to the Gentiles, in these last letters, didn't focus on the importance of preaching the Gospel. Instead his primary emphasis was on the potential of the individual believer to have a deep, personal, intimate relationship with God. He tells them there is nothing to compare with knowing Christ (Phil. 3:8). He prays that his readers may know the Lord's unknowable love (Eph. 3:19), and he instructs them to set their hearts and minds on heavenly things (Col. 3:1-2).

Too many Christians are living the kind of existence that is little more than simply hanging on until they get to glory because they haven't yet understood that the abundant life which the Lord Jesus describes in John 10:10 is for now.

We are meant to be full of joy because of our overwhelming experience of being truly, deeply, and fervently loved by the God who is Love.

As human beings, we express love in a variety of ways. In fact, recent studies have shown that different people want to have love shown to them in different ways. There are those who like to be told in words, some prefer to receive gifts, while loving touch is more important to others. Our God expresses his love for us in all these ways. He has given us a book full of words which speaks of his love, and he has given us the gift of his Son to redeem us. But he also wants to touch us deep within our spirits with a tender and profound love that we can actually feel.

We all know what it is to love and to be loved. Paul says that he wants believers to know the love of God that is so vast it is unknowable. Our experience of the love of the Lord is meant to be far superior to our experience of any human love. If it isn't, we need to take the words of Ephesians 3:16-19 and pray them for ourselves until we receive that revelation of divine love.

It is impossible to have an intimate encounter with God and not be changed. The mark of whether genuine intimacy with the Lord has occurred in prayer (or whether it is purely a self-satisfied delusion) is the extent to which the rest of our lives are different. The evidence will be a greater awareness of sin and increased desire for obedience to the Lord, more heartfelt intercession, a longing for corporate worship, a passion for scripture, and an increased, divinely inspired love for people which shows itself in practical ways.

Exercise

Ask the Lord to teach you how to pray and to plant in you the seed of a desire to pray. Don't just pray this once, pray for it daily until you begin to feel the first stirrings of that desire. Remember, you're reading this book because you want a better prayer life. This is the most fundamental exercise of all. Please don't just skip over it.

CHAPTER 3

Sacred Spaces

I must secure more time for private devotions. I have been living far too public for me. The shortening of devotions starves the soul, it grows lean and faint. I have been keeping too late hours.

(William Wilberforce)

I walked through the ancient west door of the thirteenth-century Lincoln Cathedral and what I saw created a true sense of awe. What made it so spectacular was the vast emptiness of it. Unlike every other cathedral I've visited, there were no rows of pews or chairs. Visitors were not forced to the edges of the building by roped off areas. There was simply a huge expanse of openness, the communion table at the far end with a cross on it. The awesome presence of God seemed tangible in the simplicity of that space. My first instinct was to run through the empty building and fall on my knees at the altar. Being a very shy teenager, just a few months old in the faith, I restrained myself. But that urge to run to God has never really left me.

I've never had quite the same experience in any other cathedral although there has almost invariably been a sense of standing on holy ground. I've come to understand that somehow, in a way which makes no sense to the rational mind, places which have hosted much prayer over many generations become infused with a kind of sacredness which touches the human spirit. It isn't simply the beauty of the architecture or the solemn nature of the place. It seems to be resounding echoes of encounters with God.

I have also learnt over the years that something similar happens in our own lives. In places where we pray frequently, it becomes easier to slip into the presence of God. Something about the familiarity of a place helps us to relax and keep our focus on the Lord. When I was at Bible College I, like most of the other students, shared a room, and it was very difficult to find a place where I could be alone. I was not the only one hunting down a place for a quiet time. Dozens of other students were doing the same thing. I would get up one morning and discover the ideal spot only to arrive the next day to find it occupied by someone else. I found that constantly being in different places made it much harder to fix my eyes on Jesus for that special time alone with him. For a while, my encounters with the Lord took place in a bus shelter just outside the college gates.

But even subtle changes can unsettle us. One church I know was undertaking some refurbishments. Whilst the sanctuary was not directly affected, it was necessary to temporarily reorder the worship space to allow access. This involved little more than turning the chairs the opposite way round and moving the piano from one end of the room to the other. But it changed the atmosphere. It didn't seem like quite the same church, and the connection with God didn't seem as simple. When I visited, I felt like a stranger, less at ease than before.

These experiences have convinced me that, at least when we are starting out on this journey of prayer, we need to find our own sacred space which becomes familiar to us.

Jesus said, 'When you pray, go into your room, close the door, and pray to your Father who is unseen' (Matt. 6:6).

This word *room* was rendered *closet* in old translations of the Bible and led to Christian speakers and writers referring to the *prayer closet*. When I first came across that phrase, I had images of a person huddled in the cupboard under the stairs or in a piece of bedroom furniture. I have actually wondered if this was the seed thought for CS Lewis's *Narnia* chronicles where the children enter the secret world of King Aslan through the back of a wardrobe.

Neither *room* nor *closet* adequately translate the sense of the original Greek word in this passage which is *tameion*. This word has a very particular meaning. It is used for a storeroom which would be at the heart of the house, safe from prying eyes, where household treasures would be kept. The image used by Jesus in this passage is an especially appropriate one and shows what a high value God places on solitary prayer. The prayer closet is not simply a secret place but a trove of heavenly treasure, a sacred space.

The secret place where we pray becomes a storehouse of treasure. We meet with God secretly, on our own, and this is where we are blessed beyond our wildest dreams, not blessed with material wealth but with a spiritual wealth.

Those who haven't experienced the treasures of love, joy, and peace to be found in the prayer closet may still hanker after earthly treasures. But these bring only transient pleasure. Later in Matthew 6:19-21, Jesus says,

> Do not store up for yourselves treasures on earth, where moth and rust destroy, and where thieves break in and steal. But store up for yourselves treasures in heaven, where moth and rust do not destroy, and where thieves do not break in and steal. For where your treasure is, there your heart will be also.

We often associate this passage with how we use our money as that's the next topic Jesus goes on to talk about. But his listeners would surely have made the connection with his comments about the treasure house earlier.

No one can steal from us the treasure we find in the prayer closet. We may suffer the material consequences of an economic recession, but when we pray, we can find lasting treasure which will not only bless us now but will also be a blessing to us in eternity.

So, how do we create a space for ourselves which will become that special place for our love meetings with the Lord?

It's important to say that you don't need to find somewhere that won't get used for anything else. For most of us, such a place would be a wonderful luxury. I have heard of people setting aside an entire room in their home or even constructing an outbuilding or shed for the purpose. At the opposite extreme, Susanna Wesley, mother of John and Charles, is said to have indicated to her family that she was not to be disturbed during her devotions by putting her apron over her head. What matters is not so much the place but whether you will be left alone during the time you are using it and that you feel comfortable. So a favourite armchair, the kitchen table, a desk kneeling by the bed are all common options.

In considering location, you will also want to consider posture. Many people feel they want to kneel; it helps to remind them of their need for humility before God. For others, kneeling is not practical; whilst able to get down on their knees, they would find it inordinately difficult to get up again. Sitting is perfectly acceptable as is walking about while you pray. Some people like to lie face down or bow with their head touching the floor. But I suspect most people prefer to vary their posture depending on what is happening in their heart. What we must not do is think that one position for prayer is holier than another. The aim is to ease our ability to enter the presence of God. There are no special rewards for being distracted by physical pain because we've chosen an uncomfortable posture. If lying in bed wrapped up in a duvet works for you (and doesn't simply send you to sleep), you have no need to apologise for the fact.

If you are at liberty to do so, you may wish to enhance the physical space you are using with aids to devotion. As with the choice of space, this is entirely down to what suits you. Of course, you will need your Bible, reading notes if you use them, and I always advise paper and pen (we will discuss the use of all these materials later). If you do kneel, you might want to have something to kneel on. You could choose to have a CD, mp3 player, or hymn book so you can use worship songs. People find all sorts of images helpful such as pictures with Bible verses or appropriate ornaments. Some like to light a candle or have pictures of those they are praying for. It is really up to you—if it helps you, use it; if it doesn't, ditch it.

When you first create such a space, it doesn't automatically become a *sacred* space. There is no special prayer of blessing that will turn your favourite armchair into holy ground. It is going to take time, and you are going to have to discipline yourself to use it. Routine is vital when you're endeavouring to create a new habit. Just as mountain climbing requires training and regular exercising of the body, so growing a prayer life demands determined commitment. I do not believe this can be done in a haphazard way. I have no doubt that you have to start out by making a firm appointment to meet with God at a particular place and a specific time each day. Ask anyone who has a 'successful' prayer life, and you will find they are consistent at setting aside a set time for prayer, and for the vast majority of them, it will be the first appointment of the day.

I use the term *appointment* for a reason. When you make an appointment, you stick to it. If you made an appointment to see the doctor, your accountant, or a business colleague, you would not dream of failing to turn up or even being a couple of hours late. If someone else was asking to see you at that time, you would tell them you already had a meeting scheduled, and you'd have to see them at another time. Imagine having an appointment to see the Prime Minister but giving it a miss because you needed to catch up with work. You wouldn't do it. Why on earth would you miss or delay an appointment with the King of kings? As Corrie ten Boom once said,

> Don't pray when you feel like it. Have an appointment with the
> Lord and keep it.

Your time alone with God is the most important part of each day, and the time you set aside for him is, in reality, a part of your sacred space. So fix your place and fix your time and determine you will not allow anyone or anything else to interrupt it. That time has a higher priority than doing the housework, mowing the lawn, fixing the car, or answering the phone. All the jobs will still be there when your prayer time is over, and the caller can leave a message or try again later, so don't use these things as an excuse to procrastinate. I remember hearing an Amish man say that if you give to God the first day of the week, the first part of each day and the first part of your income, you will pretty soon find God has become first in your life.

If you simply wait until you feel like praying, it will not happen. But there is power in being disciplined and sticking determinedly to the appointment we have made. RA Torrey in his excellent little book *How To Pray* says this:

> When we feel least like praying is the time when we most need to pray. We should wait quietly before God and tell Him how cold and prayerless our hearts are, and look up to Him and trust Him and expect Him to send the Holy Spirit to warm our hearts and draw them out in prayer. It will not be long before the glow of the Spirit's presence will fill our hearts, and we will begin to pray with freedom, directness, earnestness and power. Many of the most blessed seasons of prayer I have ever known have begun with a feeling of utter deadness and prayerlessness, but in my helplessness and coldness I have cast myself upon God, and looked to Him to send His Holy Spirit to teach me to pray, and He has done it.

Take encouragement from the experiences of other great saints and learn from them.

You will also find, as many others have, that whilst each of us only has twenty-four hours in any day, somehow you get more done in those days when you've prioritised prayer at the beginning. As John Wesley is reported to have said,

> I have so much to do that I spend several hours in prayer before I am able to do it.

When God first challenged me to spend more time in prayer, I was amazed to find how much more quickly I managed to get through the tasks of the rest of the day. It has been said, in the context of making financial offerings, that we cannot out-give God. The more we give, the more we receive (Luke 6:38), and I have proved that in my own life. The same appears to be true of time. I'm not suggesting you start by trying to pray for several hours each day; that would be an unrealistic goal, and you'd soon fail and become disillusioned. For now, the important thing is to set a starting time and stick to it.

Exercise

Plan your sacred space. Start by simply asking God to guide you. Then decide where it will be and how to organise it. Make an appointment with God for tomorrow and ask him to help you keep the commitment. If you use a diary, write it in like any other appointment. If you're not currently a regular prayer, just aim for fifteen to twenty minutes. If you happen to find yourself spending longer, that's fine; just don't place unrealistic expectations on yourself.

CHAPTER 4

Walking with Jesus

Jesus himself came up and walked along with them.

(Luke 24:15)

*N*ot everyone is entirely comfortable with sitting still, closing their eyes, and quietly communing with God. This does not make them less spiritual; they simply express themselves differently in worship.

There are two different kinds of people in this world, the introverts and the extroverts. We must be clear at this point that *introvert* is not a synonym for *shy*, nor is *extrovert* another word for *pushy*. In the study of personality, these two words have quite specific meanings, and it will help us to understand these in order to understand how best to develop our spiritual lives.

Broadly speaking, an introvert is someone who thrives in a quiet environment. Introverts like to think before they speak. They prefer to have just a few close friends, and they recharge their batteries by taking time to be alone in a quiet place. They may enjoy parties but find them exhausting, and they need times of quiet reflection in order to think through what they believe. So an introvert is entirely happy with the idea of sitting quietly and alone in wordless communion with God. Offer them a chance to go on retreat, and they will think they are being offered heaven on earth.

Extroverts are completely different. They love being around people and have a wide circle of friends. They feel drained if they are alone for too long and recharge their batteries by getting out with the crowd. They always want to be a part of whatever is going on. Extroverts tend to talk a lot and seem unable to process their thoughts without verbalising them. Whereas the introvert will not speak until they have decided what they believe, the extrovert will want to discuss their ideas with others in order to work out what they believe. They may start a conversation seemingly believing one thing and end up expressing the opposite view. It is not that they are changing their mind so much as making their mind up as they go whereas the introvert goes through this same process silently in their own minds. An extrovert is likely to think that a retreat would be a nightmare but invite them to a large worship event where they can be active in participation, and they will love it.

Of course, these are generalisations and, in reality, there is a sliding scale from the extreme introvert to the extreme extrovert with lots of variety in between. Most people have some extrovert and some introvert qualities or are able to learn to sometimes function within the other temperament. Preaching, for example, requires both introvert and extrovert qualities. The study and preparation required suit the introvert while the extrovert will be happier when he gets up to deliver the message he's prepared. The extrovert preacher will be drained by the study, the introvert will be drained by the delivery and would rather seek a quiet place straight after the service than stand at the door and shake hands with the members of the congregation.

When it comes to prayer, the introvert and the extrovert are comfortable with different things but, as most books are written by introverts and, consequently, most books *on prayer* are written by introverts, there is a tendency to assume that the introvert way of prayer is the only correct way to pray. This can leave extroverts feeling like failures because they cannot sit quietly for extended periods of time, and they tend to find it difficult to meditate and to appreciate the immanence of God.

We saw in the last chapter how Jesus told his disciples to go into the *prayer closet* and pray secretly there. But the verse at the start of this section tells us that Jesus communed with his disciples while they walked. This particular incident was on the road to Emmaus after the resurrection. But we also know that Jesus and his disciples walked many miles together during his earthly ministry, and they would hardly have done so in complete silence.

If you are an extrovert, your sacred space may not be a fixed spot in the home; it could be a walk around the local park, along the beach, or through the country lanes. The simple activity of walking creates a rhythm which can help some people settle into a rhythm of prayer. The extrovert is more likely to be prompted to praise and worship by being in the heart of God's creation and seeing its glory than by meditating on a passage of scripture. The vastness of the sky, the elegance of a heron, the simple beauty of a crocus, the thunder of a waterfall can each speak to us of the nature of God and inspire awe and wonder at their creator.

> For since the creation of the world God's invisible qualities—His eternal power and divine nature—have been clearly seen, being understood from what has been made, so that men are without excuse. (Rom. 1:20)

God speaks through the book of creation as well as his written Word.

Extroverts may well find it difficult to pray alone and find it beneficial to be part of a group of two or three who meet frequently to pray together. They may find that participating in some form of activity, perhaps an artistic or creative one, helps them to pray. The old fashioned ladies' knitting circle in churches was not such a bad idea. Some particularly artistic extroverts have used music or even painting as a medium for prayer. I imagine the carpenter's workshop in

Nazareth saw a great deal of prayer. The key for extroverts, even more so than for introverts, is to experiment and find what works for you.

Exercise

Whether you regard yourself as an extrovert or an introvert, try this exercise. Take a walk in your neighbourhood. If there is some green space or a park near your home, you might like to go there, or you can simply walk around the streets. You might want to go with a friend or a small group. As you walk, look for evidences of the majesty of God in creation. What does the weather tell you about God? Do the plants, animals, or birds reveal anything about his nature? Pray for the people you pass or those in the houses along the road. Do you feel prompted by God to pray for any of these people in a particular way? When you get home, reflect on the walk—was there a common thread to your thoughts and prayers? Might God be speaking to you through this and asking you to do something practical?

CHAPTER 5

Here I Am

> Now Samuel did not yet know the Lord: the word of the Lord had
> not yet been revealed to him.
>
> (1 Sam. 3:7)

It is fundamentally important that we understand that knowing God through prayer is a matter of revelation. No doubt many other people climbed Mount Moriah but didn't hear from God as Abraham did. Many would have stood where the disciples were but had not seen Jesus in his glory. On its own, going up the mountain was simply an exercise, but the Lord chose to reveal himself there.

We know the account of Samuel's boyhood very well. His mother, Hannah, could not conceive, so she pleaded with God for a child and promised to give him back to the Lord when he answered her prayer. Hannah's prayer was so fervent that Eli the priest thought she was drunk. This was a woman praying with her entire being. After God answered her prayer and Samuel was weaned (which would have been at about two years of age), she took him to the house of the Lord at Shiloh where she dedicated him and handed him over to Eli. She was a most remarkable woman of intense faith, courage, and integrity.

Samuel lived in the tabernacle. He was involved in the ministry (1 Sam. 2:18). He saw the ritual and the sacrifices, he heard the prayers, he even slept close to the Ark of the Covenant where God's presence dwelt between the cherubim (1 Sam. 3:1-3). Surely Samuel would have had a personal relationship with God as many of his ancestors had done. We know the story. Samuel hears a voice calling him and thinks it is the old man Eli. He responds, but it isn't Eli. It happens again with the same result. And then we are told, 'Samuel did not yet know the Lord: the word of the Lord had not yet been revealed to him' (verse 7). Samuel didn't recognise God's voice because, despite living so close to his presence, God had not revealed himself to Samuel.

There was a time, before I became a Christian, when I was searching for God. I went to church on Sundays, I prayed every day, and read my Bible. I believed with all my heart, and my desire was to know God. And yet I didn't know him. The Bible I was reading every day was, in reality, a closed book to me—I could make no sense of it. Then came the glorious moment when my spiritual eyes were opened. God revealed himself to me, and the Holy Spirit brought life to his Word. One moment I didn't know the Lord, the next I did.

There is an important lesson for us here as we begin our journey into the mountains of prayer—we are dependent on God to reveal himself. Just settling ourselves to pray does not mean we are going to automatically hear God's voice. Unlike us, God isn't in a hurry. He has all the time in eternity. One reason we don't hear him speaking is because we don't take the time to stop and be still. Even when Samuel heard God's voice, he was dashing around. Eli, though lacking in wisdom in the way he dealt with the pilgrims coming to Shiloh and with disciplining his own sons, actually got this bit right when he instructed Samuel, 'Go and lie down, and if He calls you, say, Speak Lord for your servant is listening' (verse 9).

Samuel followed Eli's instruction, and the Word of the Lord was indeed revealed to him. From that day on, he knew God.

The great writer on prayer, Andrew Murray, said,

> Take time in the inner chamber to bow down and worship, and wait
> on Him until He unveils Himself.

Our private devotions will be transformed if only we will take that time during our worship to say, as Samuel did, 'Here I am . . . speak Lord . . . I'm listening.'

But what does that mean in practice?

The account of Samuel illustrates God's desire to speak to anyone who will take seriously the business of listening to him. That is because, sadly, so few believers actually try to hear his voice. He spoke to a young boy, Samuel, because even though he was trying to speak to Eli and his sons, they weren't paying attention (1 Sam. 2:12-36). God will speak to those who genuinely want to hear, but we must prove ourselves to be diligent seekers of him (Heb. 11:6). So it is no good simply dashing into his presence saying, 'Here I am' and expecting an immediate reply, giving up after five minutes and never trying again. We must take our time and live up to our commitment to go to our sacred space daily to seek the face of God.

Even so, I have found the Lord to be remarkably unpredictable when it comes to this business of unveiling himself. There have been times when I have become intensely aware of his voice and his presence within moments of settling into my prayer time. But there have also been other times when I have spent an hour in worship, and only in the last five minutes has he spoken to me. This unpredictability is not caprice—it ensures that we don't fall into the trap of thinking we can control God. He sovereignly makes himself known according to his own will and is not to be *summoned up* by manipulating mortals.

No, we must take time to watch and wait, and as we do so, we must worship. We are not collecting sightings of God as an ornithologist might watch for birds or a fan might wait for their favourite celebrity. We are entering into the Holy of Holies, so worship with humility is paramount.

Exercise

As you begin this part of the journey, you may find it helpful to use one of the devotions at the end of this book. Turn to the first one, *Jesus I Long To See Your Face*, which is especially appropriate for beginners as it may be spoken or sung to a number of different hymn tunes if desired. When you have read it, you should simply stop and be still for a few moments. Wait for a little while and simply enjoy the peace. Then thank Jesus for being with you.

CHAPTER 6

My Sheep Know My Voice

God's voice is still and quiet and easily buried under an avalanche of clamour.

(Charles Stanley)

Many Christians, when they start to think seriously about the possibility of having God speak to them, wonder how they can be sure they are hearing his voice and not that of their own mind or even of the forces of darkness. But Jesus was very clear on the matter, 'my sheep listen to my voice' (John 10:27). In the first half of John chapter 10, Jesus explains that he is the Good Shepherd and that the sheep recognise the shepherd's voice (verse 4).

The way this comes about on the hillside is that the shepherd continually talks to his sheep so that they very quickly come to distinguish his voice from that of any other shepherd. They are with him all the time, so they are familiar with the way he speaks.

If we want to learn the sound of the Good Shepherd's voice, then we need to constantly put ourselves in the place where he speaks, and he does that most clearly and most commonly through his written Word, the Bible. It is so important that we familiarise ourselves with scripture because God speaks to us directly through his Word. But it also provides us with a plumb line for measuring everything else we might think God could be saying to us. We cannot excuse an adulterous affair or theft at the workplace by saying that God told us it was okay because these are clearly contrary to the will of God as expressed in the Ten Commandments. If we hear a voice telling us otherwise, it is not the voice of the Good Shepherd. Everything God says agrees with the Bible, so it is vital that we know it and begin to learn the sound of his voice through it. It needs to be read consistently, day by day, and we need to read all of it, not just the parts we like.

But God does not speak to us only through his Word. He has also sent the Holy Spirit, 'who will teach you all things' (John 14:26). He often speaks directly to our hearts. This is experienced by different people in different ways, so it really is something you have to grow into for yourself. But within the context of a personal prayer time, I believe most people hear the voice of God as a gentle 'knowing' in their heart. Although many people will express their experience with the words, 'God said to me . . .' it is exceptional for someone to hear an audible voice or see a vision. Some find words or phrases falling fully formed into their minds, some get the feeling they should look up a particular passage of scripture, some see images forming in their imagination, some will have an idea and experience a particular peace or certainty that they should act on it.

All this may sound a bit wishy-washy when you haven't yet experienced this for yourself, so I'd like to tell you about how my husband, Steve, began to understand about hearing God. He prayed a very simple prayer, 'Lord, teach me the sound of your voice.' At that time, he was a young man hosting a prayer triplet on Tuesday nights, and the other two friends were extremely inconsistent in their timekeeping as young men can often be. Steve began to have the feeling that someone was telling him when to put the kettle on, so he decided to act on the inner prompting. When he did so, the kettle boiled as his friends arrived at the door. Sometimes he wasn't sure whether he was just imagining it and didn't put the kettle on. The two young men would arrive a few minutes later at just the time the kettle would have boiled. In this very simple and very ordinary way, Steve began to learn the sound of the Lord's voice so he could recognise it in less trivial circumstances.

Here's another example. 'Why does the Lord tell me about such trivial things?' This was a question posed to me by an elderly lady who had been visiting her niece. She had thought she heard the Lord tell her that a particular house in the road would be put up for sale. She said nothing, but a couple of weeks later, the niece phoned and mentioned that there was now a house for sale in their street. 'It wouldn't be number 5, would it?' the aunt asked. The niece was astonished. 'How did you know that?' The Lord was teaching this elderly lady the sound of his voice. By hearing him talk about unimportant and insignificant details, she was learning what the Lord's voice sounds like. Then when he has something important to tell her, she will be able to recognise who is speaking to her.

Our God is very gracious. He always starts where we are and teaches us in a way we can understand. It's unlikely that he will teach you by telling you when to put the kettle on or telling you in advance when a house is going up for sale. But he may well prompt you to do apparently trivial things and bring about unexpected outcomes so that you find yourself saying, 'Well, I suppose it must have been God telling me to do that.' As you experience God directing you in your day-to-day life, you will also begin to recognise the same voice speaking to you in your prayer time.

Exercise

Read John 10:1-15. Ask Jesus to teach you the sound of his voice. Remember that he is always saying, 'I love you.' Listen for the still small voice whispering those words to your heart. It is there; you simply need to learn to recognise the sound. You may not recognise it the first time you do this exercise, or even the second or the third. But if you will do this consistently, taking time to be quiet and diligently seeking him, you will gradually come to hear those precious words for yourself.

CHAPTER 7

Mind Control

Whatever is true, whatever is noble, whatever is right, whatever
is pure, whatever is lovely, whatever is admirable—if anything is
excellent or praiseworthy—think about such things.

(Phil. 4:8)

We are so used to noise in our world that being quiet and focusing
on God has become extremely difficult for most of us. Even if our exterior world
is quiet—no music, no TV, no conversation, no traffic noise—we always seem
to have the sound of our own voice inside our head.

Most of us believe we have no choice about what we think. All sorts of
strange ideas pop into our heads, and we just let them sit there and grow like
weeds. We allow our minds to wander wherever they want to go. Sometimes
there are X-rated movies showing behind our eyes, and we indulge them
because no one else knows. But it isn't the sort of thing that should be viewed
in the temple of the Holy Spirit, and we don't have to let these things control
us. The Bible tells us that we are to be transformed by the renewing of our

minds. In fact, Paul goes on to say that this is how we get to understand God's will in Romans 12:2:

> Do not conform any longer to the pattern of this world, but be transformed by the renewing of your mind. Then you will be able to test and approve what God's will is—his good, pleasing and perfect will.

In my experience, there are three different kinds of intrusive thoughts which tend to distract us from fixing our eyes on Jesus during our prayer times, and each needs to be tackled in a different way.

The first of these is the utterly mundane and is typified by such things as, 'I must remember to get milk when I go out later'. These are so easy to deal with they need never be a serious problem. When such thoughts come, simply take a piece of paper and a pen and write them down so you can deal with them after your prayer time. Once you've done that, you can return to your devotions without worrying whether you'll remember.

The second is at the opposite end of the spectrum and includes all those thoughts you'd be ashamed to have broadcast in public. I want to encourage you by revealing that everyone has to deal with this. It is one of the devil's favourite ways of causing us to stumble. You may think that no one else is so perverted that they have to deal with the kind of images which pour unbidden into your mind. That's another of the devil's lies—he tries it on everyone. I'm sure that the reason Paul wrote Philippians 4:8 (above) was because he knew what this was like, and he'd found the solution.

We have to make a conscious decision, when these dreadful thoughts come to our minds, to change our thinking. It's no good just trying not to think about them. That's like trying not to think of an elephant—once the idea is there, no matter how hard you try, it's not going away unless you think about something else. There are plenty of noble, pure, and lovely things to think about. Have some pictures of the natural world, God's creation, to focus on and praise him for his handiwork, read some Psalms, sing a worship song, or use one of the devotions from this book.

But don't just do this in your prayer time; do it in the rest of your life. I have found that the more disciplined I am with my thought life in general, the fewer problems I have when it comes to prayer. When you're not in the time you've set aside to spend alone with the Lord, it is easier to deal with these thoughts because you can simply go off and do something else, anything which is absorbing and requires concentration.

> The best way to be rid of bad thoughts in my prayers is not to receive them out of my prayers. (Thomas Fuller)

We have to be so careful what we feed our minds with. If you watch sex scenes on TV, don't be surprised if they come back to you when you're trying to pray. If you listen to foul language in so-called comedy radio programmes, don't be surprised if those words keep coming to mind. We live in a world where we are surrounded by many unholy images and where our culture is counter to that of the Gospel, so we will inevitably be polluted against our will. But let's not add to that by our own foolishness. Let us strive to be holy so that we are temples where God's Spirit is comfortable to dwell.

Finally, there are those distractions which may not be distractions at all. These are the kind of things: the image of a friend we haven't seen for ages pops into our mind, we suddenly think about an item we've heard on the news, we hear an ambulance siren and wonder what is wrong. While it may not be the case, it is distinctly possible that these are promptings from the Lord to pray. You have nothing to lose, so the best thing to do is to turn these distractions to prayer. Pray for the friend, for their health, for their spiritual progress, for their family, for protection, pray about that news item, for those affected by it, for peace in the situation, pray for whoever is at the other end of the ambulance call-out, pray the paramedics will get there in time, that they will know how best to treat the patient. When you've prayed, tell the Lord you are trusting him with the situation and move on. If these random thoughts are actually the devil trying to stop you from praying, you will deal him a heavy blow by turning his weapon back on himself.

None of these wanderings of the mind need to disturb you greatly. Please don't get frustrated with yourself. We all have to deal with these things. Sometimes they are more of a problem, sometimes less. But the most important thing is that you don't allow them to prevent you from pressing on with worship.

Just one final thought on this subject of controlling our thinking. Some religions teach that people need to empty their minds in order to have an encounter with God. In fact, the reverse is true. Nowhere in the Bible are we told to empty our minds. To empty one's mind is to open it up to all sorts of dubious influences. No, the fruit of the Spirit is *self*-control (Gal. 5:23), and we are to be in control of our own thinking, not clearing out all thoughts but focusing them on our lovely Lord Jesus.

Exercise

> We take captive every thought to make it obedient to Christ. (2 Cor. 10:5)

It is a good idea to decide in advance what you are going to do in order to take those intrusive thoughts captive. You need anything wholesome that will distract you, but words of scripture can be particularly effective. Ask God to help you find the right thing for you to focus on when you need to change your thinking. Then spend some time thinking of as many verses of scripture as you can which you could meditate on when necessary. Choose a few and write them down in your notebook so you can refer to them when required. You will soon find you have memorised them!

CHAPTER 8

Meditation

If we then let the words of Christ abide in us, they will stir us up in prayer.

(RA Torrey)

One of my favourite autobiographies is the account of a devout Hindu who became a Christian, *Death of a Guru* by Rabindranath Maharaj. I would thoroughly recommend it to anyone who wants to understand more about the gulf of difference between Eastern mysticism and Christian spirituality because he has known both and shares his experiences with great honesty.

There are Christians who have become sidetracked down the route of Eastern-style meditation. Some accounts I have read of such ventures sound remarkably like the experiences of Maharaj while he was practising Hindu meditation. Consequently there is a backlash in some quarters of the Evangelical community against what is, in the Christian tradition, known as contemplative prayer and which can appear to share some characteristics with Eastern meditation. It is important, therefore, that we understand the primary and fundamental difference between Christian and Eastern meditation.

Hindu meditation is practised by emptying the mind in order to gain a higher consciousness and ultimately to experience nirvana or *nothingness*. Christian meditation is not about emptying the mind but about filling it with thoughts of God, and this is best done by contemplating scripture.

The Apostle Paul says, *'Let the word of Christ dwell in you richly'* (Col. 3:16), and this beautifully describes the act of Christian meditation. In Psalm 119, the writer says, *'I have hidden Your word in my heart'* (verse 11), *'I meditate on Your precepts'* (verse 15) and prays, *'open my eyes that I may see wonderful things in Your law'* (verse 18).

Christian meditation is about prayerfully absorbing scripture into our very being, and there are a number of practices which can help us to do that.

The first is memorising. When we memorise a single verse or a longer passage of scripture, it becomes available to us when we need it. Because we have lodged it in our brain, it comes to mind in the right circumstances. There are countless times in my life when I have faced temptation or needed a Word from God, and a memorised passage has come to mind which has been pertinent to the situation. Memorising takes discipline, and the older we get, the more discipline seems to be required to fix new things in our heads.

I have heard it said that about the age of seven is the best time to learn by memorising as that is the age at which the brain is particularly receptive to learning by rote. That is why traditional education had us all reciting our 'timetables' in primary school. If you have responsibility of children in that age group, it's a great opportunity to teach them scriptures that will stay in their minds the whole of their lives. The rest of us will have to work harder at it, but repeat a scripture often enough, and it will stick.

For some reason, it seems that words set to music are easier to remember. My youngest son still remembers Proverbs 3:5 because he was taught it with a catchy tune, some at a holiday club, when he was about seven or eight. Over the years, I have put various pieces of scripture to simple tunes to help me remember them, from single verses to whole Psalms. They are not tunes I would boast about as I am no musician, but they have enabled me to memorise passages which are helpful to me.

The second practice I want to mention is what I call mulling over scripture. Like a cow with the cud, we can take a verse or two and, instead of just assuming we know what it means, we can chew it over in our mind, turning it around to look at it from different angles, thinking about what each of the words means. For example, 1 Peter 1:16 quotes several Old Testament passages—*be holy, because I am holy*. What *is* holiness? What does it mean that *God* is holy? How can *I* be holy? I am not told to *become* holy but to *be* holy, so what are the implications of that? We have to be careful that when we answer these questions, we do so in the light of other passages of scripture and not with our own bright ideas. But as we explore scripture in this way, we will come to understand it more fully. This practice can be particularly beneficial with those passages of scripture that have become overly familiar to us because we've read them so many times. If you find yourself skipping over a passage quickly because you think you know it so well, slow down, take a phrase or two, and mull over them. You may be surprised by the new light which is shed on them.

The third form of meditation I want to mention is imagining. By this, I don't mean making things up, but rather taking a passage of the Bible, usually from the Gospels, and using your imagination to place yourself within the scene described. There is a principle of learning which is expressed in the following way: I hear and I forget, I see and I remember, I do and I understand. By taking a passage such as Luke 8:40-56, the healing of the sick woman and Jairus's daughter, and using our imagination to place ourselves in the crushing crowds and follow the events as they unfold, we can gain a deeper insight into the intensity of the emotions involved, the pain and joy experienced by the participants, and the awe of the bystanders at the power of Jesus to intervene in life-changing ways. The passage speaks more powerfully to us. Something which has seemed so familiar becomes fresh and new.

When you think about it, this is what the media of film does all the time. Filmmakers take words and turn them into images on the screen—they take the place of our imagination and do the hard work for us in creating the pictures. We are just as capable of recreating those scenes from scripture in our own mind as a director of a film might. We can very easily go the extra few yards and do this for ourselves with the Bible passages we are reading, bringing the characters to life and getting to understand why they acted as they did.

Exercise

We are all overfamiliar with the twenty-third Psalm. Take this psalm and meditate on it. Put yourself in the place of the sheep and imagine yourself on the hillside with the Good Shepherd. Consider each sentence one by one and ponder what it means for the sheep and their relationship with the Shepherd. How does this translate itself into your relationship with Jesus? How does this make you feel?

CHAPTER 9

Waiting on God

The giver is more than the gift; God is more than the blessing. And,
our being kept waiting on Him is the only way for our learning to
find our life and joy in Himself.

(Andrew Murray)

*T*here are some of the current *name it and claim it* school of prayer
whose only explanation for us not receiving immediate answers to our requests
is a lack of faith on our part. According to their theology, you can have whatever
you ask for in prayer. This, of course, is only a partial theology and so is flawed.
We will look at praying for things later as this is an important part of the prayer
life, but the main purpose of prayer is not to ask God for things but to dwell in
his presence. If we don't get that part of our relationship with him right, all the
stuff we ask for is irrelevant.

God's priorities are not the same as ours. If the only way our heavenly Father
can get our attention is by withholding from us the things we ask for so that
we keep coming back to him, then he will do this. The delay in receiving an

answer may not be a lack of faith, or a misunderstanding of God's will, or sinful behaviour (these are the usual explanations for unanswered prayer). It may simply be that the Lord wants us to spend time in his company, and the only way some of us will do that is if we are feeling needy and want something.

We don't really need the vast majority of the things we ask God for. Paul recognised that the greatest needs of believers were spiritual. When we look at his letters and read of the prayers he prayed for those under his apostolic care, we see nothing about physical needs being met. Instead we see phrases such as, *to give you spiritual wisdom and insight* or *that your hearts will be flooded with light,* or *that you may experience the love of Christ* (Eph. 1:17, 18, 3:19).

If only we could get our thoughts away from the material world and all its troubles for a few moments and fix our eyes on Jesus as the writer to the Hebrews exhorts us (12:2), we would find not only our prayer lives transformed, but also our ability to cope with the day-to-day troubles that so easily drag us down.

Ask a persecuted Christian how you can best pray for them, and very often they will not ask for relief from their sufferings but for patience and endurance. This is because they have learnt, like Paul, that there is a fellowship with Christ through sharing in suffering (Phil. 3:10). Most of us would rather have the quick fix than learn intimacy with God through leaning on him in our struggles.

But if we can learn not only to wait for God, but also to wait upon God, and to accept his comfort in our trials we will find, as Andrew Murray says, that God is more than the blessing, and that we would rather have fellowship with him than answers to our requests for the material and physical things that loom so large when our spiritual eyes slip away from gazing intently upon Jesus.

> Oh, if God's children only knew what a glorious God they have, and what a privilege it is to be linked in fellowship with Him, then they would rejoice in Him! (Andrew Murray)

Waiting on God is possibly the most neglected aspect of prayer.

Because most of us are happier talking than listening, we take this into our prayer times. We present ourselves with our requests and maybe some confession, thanksgiving, or praise, but we do not have the inclination to sit and wait. Yet for those who have learnt the secret of waiting upon God, it becomes an essential part not only of prayer, but of daily life.

Dick Eastman in *The Hour That Changes the World* describes waiting as *wordless worship* or *silent soul surrender*. It is the single most important thing we can do to develop intimacy with God. The psalmist wrote, 'Be still and know that I am God' (Ps. 46:10).

> The Hebrew word for 'still' is raphah, which means to cease; let alone; become weak, feeble. It is from the root rapha, which means to mend and be made thoroughly whole by the hand of a physician. (David Wilkerson)

Waiting is the key to wholeness and to answered prayer. In Psalm 40:1, David says, '*I waited patiently for the Lord; He turned to me and heard my cry.*' Waiting is the way to find spiritual refreshing as those who wait on the Lord will renew their strength (Isa. 40:31).

In his little book *Breaking Through in Prayer*, Dan Chesney says this,

> The Hebrew word for 'wait' in Isaiah 40:31 is 'qaveh' which means 'to twist or bind together'. Therefore, as we are waiting (fellowshipping) upon the Lord, our lives are being twisted or bound up together. Christ is literally being melded into our being. The nature, abilities, characteristics and substances of Christ become intertwined with our recreated human spirit.

This is a beautiful image and is the key to becoming more Christlike. Spending five minutes waiting on the Lord will do more to develop your true godliness than many hours striving to do the right thing and keeping all those pharisaical laws we tend to make up for ourselves. In reality, we can't do anything ourselves.

Apart from me you can do nothing. (John 15:5)

One afternoon my youngest son, who was eleven years old at the time, came out of school and announced, 'We started World War II today.' Having three boys, I know their ability to create chaos, but I think even together they would find it difficult to cause global conflict.

Of course, my son didn't actually mean what he'd said, but something quite different. However, it does seem to me that we often like to claim credit for things that turn out well while blaming someone else, (the devil, the husband, the worship leader, the prime minister, perhaps even God) when things don't go according to plan.

For example, when we've felt the touch of God in our hearts during a service, it's because we are spiritually in tune, free from sin, praying more than everyone else. When we don't feel a buzz during the worship time, it's because the pastor chose the wrong hymns, the guitar was out of tune, or the person behind us kept coughing.

Actually, none of these is the case. We experience the Lord because he is gracious enough to reveal himself to us.

We can make the same mistake with our ministries. We want to be recognised for the number of people we've witnessed to, the impact we've had on those we've visited, the loving acts we've performed. We forget what the Apostle Paul said to the Ephesians in chapter 4 verses 11 to 12, that it is the Lord who raises up people for ministry—*He* gave some to be . . .

I was brought up short by the Lord once when I was struggling to put a sermon together. After five hours, I still wasn't confident that I had the right message for the congregation. A good friend reminded me that it was God's responsibility to speak to his people not mine. I repented of my pride and arrogance in thinking I had to do a good job in order for them to hear him and asked for the Lord's anointing.

You'd have to ask someone else whether God spoke to people that morning, but I got the message. If the Holy Spirit doesn't show up, it doesn't matter how eloquent I am. People's hearts will not be changed.

Jesus said, 'Apart from me you can do nothing.' We would prefer that he had said, 'Apart from me you can do some things, but if you want any help just call.' Until we recognise that Jesus actually meant what he said and said what he meant, the outcome of our efforts to please him will be patchy at best.

This is particularly true of prayer. We pray many prayers that seem to go unanswered. We see results which are contrary to what we prayed. Sick people decline instead of getting better, marriages fail, loved ones die without apparently professing faith. There is no standard answer we can give to explain these things, except this: Jesus said, 'If you abide in me and my words abide in you, ask whatever you wish and it will be given to you' (John 15:7).

The thing is that unless we are abiding in Christ, waiting on Him, being bound up with Him, we will never be clear what it is to pray according to His will (Matt. 6:10).

Exercise

Don't even try to begin the day without turning your eyes and fixing them on Jesus. Not everyone has sufficient mental alertness for a full-blown quiet time first thing in the morning. But it is perfectly possible to fellowship with the Lord, even before you've managed to open your eyes, if your heart is set on him. So make it your daily practice to turn your thoughts to the Lord even before you get out of bed, acknowledging that apart from him you can do nothing. Set aside part of your quiet time each day simply for waiting on God. Ask him to teach you about abiding in him so that you can learn to live and pray in such a way that it brings glory to him.

CHAPTER 10

The Flesh Is Weak

> By perseverance the snail reached the ark.
>
> (CH Spurgeon)

When you want to pray, have you ever noticed that 'the spirit is willing but the body is weak' (Matt. 26:41)? Jesus said these words in Gethsemane to Peter when asking him to pray. I've always thought of it in this way, 'Peter, you need to pray so that you have the strength to do what you know is right.' But perhaps the Lord was explaining to Peter why he was finding it hard to pray. It wasn't that Peter didn't want to pray but that, in his tiredness, his physical body was rebelling against the idea.

It is probably universally true that when we try to change our behaviour from a negative pattern to a positive one, our flesh cries out against it. It could be eating more healthily, taking more exercise, giving up smoking, watching less TV, getting our tongue under control. Whatever it is, we may be very sincere in our desire for change, but our body craves the taste of the chocolate, longs to put the feet up on the couch, and share that little titbit of gossip (just for prayer you understand).

So it shouldn't surprise us that when it comes to something as important as prayer our flesh tells us we really would be happier doing just about anything else. The problem we all face is the power struggle between our body and our spirit to see which is really in control. The first stage in gaining the victory is to recognise that we are spirits which happen to live in a body. It is the spirit who should be in control and not the body. You will never find true joy, and you will never develop a powerful prayer life as long as the body is dictating the terms of the relationship. That's why Paul says, 'Offer your bodies as living sacrifices' (Rom. 12:1).

Getting our body into line is part of our worship and a prerequisite for becoming a prayer.

Here's an example. At the time of writing, almost every day in the past month it has rained. When it's time for my prayer walk, my flesh starts telling me how much it doesn't want to get wet and cold and how it would much rather sit down with a mug of hot chocolate and a good book. At this point, I have a choice. I can give in and do what my body wants and neglect my spirit. Or I can tell my body that the walk will do it good and get on with doing what I know will nourish my spirit and give me the space I need to intercede for those on my prayer list. It's like disciplining a child—each time it gets a little easier to do the right thing, but give in once, and you're back to square one.

It's not easy to get up half an hour earlier to fit in a quiet time before going to work, it's not easy to go to the prayer meeting every week, it's not easy to commit to praying for your church leaders on a daily basis, it's not easy to take time to be quiet and listen to God. In fact, anything to do with prayer is not going to be easy. It requires utter commitment and determination. That's why Paul claimed, 'I discipline my body like an athlete, training it to do what it should' (1 Cor. 9:27). It takes time and effort. But if we will persevere and not give up, our flesh will come into line, submit to our spirit and our prayer lives will be transformed.

It has been said that it takes six weeks to develop a new habit. In my personal experience, it often takes a lot longer, especially in spiritual matters. If you are aware that the grumblings of the flesh are restricting the development of your prayer life, make a conscious decision to put your spirit in control and to persist with the self-discipline required to develop a new habit. It's not good enough to say you are going to give it a try. That leaves a loophole for the flesh. The only thing that works is to make a firm decision and determine to see it through whatever happens.

Possibly the issue most of us have the biggest problem with is tiredness. Do you ever find yourself falling asleep when you pray? I've found prayer so effective at making me drop off that on those occasions when I wake in the night and can't get back to sleep, I begin to pray for members of our church. Very often, I'm asleep before I've prayed for a handful of people.

I think there are three main reasons why prayer and sleepiness go together. The first of these explains the situation I've just outlined. We have an enemy who doesn't want us to pray. Prayer is an act of warfare in the spiritual battle that rages around us, and the devil wants to stop us. He will do all he can, and one of his methods is to make us feel sleepy so that we cannot concentrate. That's why I sometimes walk when I pray.

Another reason why we get sleepy during prayer is that the vitality has gone out of our quiet times: little acts of disobedience mar our relationship with the Lord, a never changing routine can become dry and stale, failure to learn a lesson means we can't move forward. We have to do all we can to avoid creating meaningless ritual and to keep our prayer lives fresh. But above all, we must make sure there is no sin or rebellion in our lives which is inhibiting the relationship between us and our heavenly Father.

The third reason we become sleepy in our prayer times is simply because we're tired! Most people in Western society are sleep deprived. The average person today gets about two hours less sleep a night than was typical 100 years ago. Being a person of prayer means being alert, and that requires appropriate times of sleep. Yes, I know the stories about John Wesley getting up at four o'clock in the morning to pray, but do you think he was up until midnight watching TV or chatting on social networking sites?

Not only do we need sleep, but we need to obey our Maker's instructions and actually take a day off each week. For many Christians, Sunday is their busiest and most tiring day. If that's the case for you and you work for five of the other days of the week and spend the sixth on housework or DIY, you need to think seriously about how to apply the scriptural injunctions about keeping Sabbath. I once heard a preacher lament the number of times Christians complain about being tired but never say how much they are looking forward to the refreshment of their day off. Is that you?

Exercise

Most adults have a pretty good idea about what time of day they function best. For some, it is early in the morning, for others, it may be during the afternoon or late evening. As far as you are able to move your main prayer time as close as possible to the time of day, you feel most alert. Also think carefully about whether you are getting enough rest and sleep and consider modifying your lifestyle. You will find such changes affect your general sense of well-being and your physical health as well as your relationship with God.

CHAPTER 11

Don't Look Back

Or suppose a king is about to go to war against another king. Will he not first sit down and consider whether he is able with ten thousand men to oppose the one coming against him with twenty thousand? If he is not able, he will send a delegation while the other is still a long way off and will ask for terms of peace. In the same way, any of you who does not give up everything he has cannot be my disciple.

(Luke 14:31-33)

A Pentecostal minister I know told me how he had once stopped his congregation in the middle of a hymn because they were singing words he knew they didn't mean. He had tried to set up a Saturday morning prayer meeting, and the people had not responded. Yet on Sunday, there they were, singing, 'Here I am, wholly available.'

Why do we do this? Why do we sing songs with words we don't mean? Perhaps we're not thinking about the words, but we like the tune. Maybe we are being carried along by emotion—we really do mean the words at the moment we are singing them, but get us outside of church, and the enthusiasm fades.

Sometimes, it's that our fear of man is greater than our fear of God, and we're more concerned about what people around us will think if we don't sing, than what God thinks about the difference between what we say and what's in our hearts.

But to me, the more interesting question is why are we not wholly available to God? Why do we set out on the Christian life but not live it wholeheartedly? And particularly, why do we set out to improve our prayer life but drift away after a few weeks or even days?

I think the answer to that has something to do with the fact that we don't know the Lord well enough to fully trust him. We're afraid that if we do make ourselves wholly available, he will ask us to do things we don't want to do. I've heard people express the fear that the Lord might call them to the mission field in a remote and underdeveloped part of the world. There are all sorts of fears—fear of being called to open-air preaching, fear of not being permitted to marry, fear of being told to give everything away and live in poverty. We all have fears, and the devil plays on these to try to make us think that the Lord will tell us to do things that will be uncomfortable or embarrassing. This can be very effective at limiting our prayer lives because we become afraid of listening to God for fear of what he might say.

In Psalm 37:4, David says, 'Take delight in the Lord, and He will give you your heart's desires' (NLT). This is a two-edged promise. On first reading, it seems to be a simple counter to the fear that God will ask us to do things we don't want to do. It appears to be saying that if we delight in the Lord we will receive the things we really want. We just have to work out how to take delight in the Lord, and then we'll have the key to answered prayer. But there is much more to this verse because there is a dynamic we miss as we rush towards the words 'heart's desire' and start thinking about all the things we'd really like to have.

David says, 'Take delight in the Lord.' We take delight in the Lord by spending time with him, reading his Word, praying, and worshipping. As we do this, we are changed, transformed, to become more like Jesus. Part of that transformation occurs within the desires we have in our hearts. Things which once seemed important to us slip away into the shadows as our priorities change, and we fall in love with Jesus. The old desires fade, and we find that God himself is planting new desires in our hearts. He literally gives to us the desires which then take root in our hearts. Where we were once enthralled by sin, we want holiness; the obsession with material wealth gives way to a desire to build up a storehouse of treasure in heaven. Boredom with church is replaced with a desire to spend time with our brothers and sisters in the Lord.

There is no need for fear of what God will ask us to do because, if we are delighting in him, he works to transform our desires to conform with his will. That is not to say that it will always be easy to do what God wants, but when he asks something challenging of us and we look within ourselves for our response, we will always find there is a seed of desire within our hearts to be obedient to him that will enable us to do whatever he asks. But then, we have to put it into practice, and holiness is the one thing where it is most difficult to get our actions to line up with our heart's desire.

It is easy for us to delude ourselves about our true desires. I once wanted a particular outcome to a problem, but when it was resolved, I was actually disappointed. What I thought I wanted was completely different to what I found in my heart when the whole episode was over. We've talked about the Lord giving us the desires of our hearts and how he works with us to transform our desires so that they conform to his will. But that is only part of the story. Sometimes we simply have to make an active decision to submit our wills to the will of God.

The concept, 'thy will be done' occurs in more than one place in scripture, and the circumstances are quite different.

It appears as a line in the Lord's Prayer where Jesus instructs as to pray, 'Your kingdom come, Your will be done on earth as it is in heaven' (Matt. 6:10). Though we shouldn't treat this prayer as a ritual, it is intended as a guide for us, of the bases we should cover in our personal devotions.

In this context, 'Your will be done' indicates an ongoing attitude of heart. We are to pray continually that God's sovereign will should be fulfilled in our own lives and the lives of the people around us. To pray this prayer is to put ourselves in a place of submission to God for it says, 'Lord, reign in me and in my world, day by day.'

We sometimes use this little phrase, 'Your will be done' when we pray because we don't know whether what we're asking for is, in fact, the will of God. We have to be careful about what we mean when we say it. If we mean 'This is what I would really like but if it's not what's best for me, please don't let me have it', then that is a mature approach to prayer. But if we mean 'It would be nice to have this, but I don't really expect you will give it to me', then we are being childish (which is not the same as childlike) and not praying in faith.

Having taught this little prayer to the disciples, Jesus himself makes use of it in Gethsemane where he is battling to submit his will to that of the Father in a very specific set of circumstances, 'Yet not my will, but Yours be done' (Luke 22:42). None of us will ever understand what it cost the Lord Jesus. But he was able to make that one-off act of submission and say, 'Your will be done', precisely because he had been practising living in the will of God all his life.

If we are to take the difficult situations in our lives and submit to the will of God ourselves, we will have to develop a lifestyle of submission in the details of daily life. If we don't do that, when the crisis hits us, our instinct will be to rebel, and we will have a really hard time getting our flesh to do the right thing.

It's all about learning to trust God (Prov. 3:5). My experience has shown me my need to trust that God does work all things together for our good (Rom. 8:28). I don't even know my own heart, so how can I possibly know what is best for me? That's why God reveals himself to us as our heavenly Father. It really is a case of, 'Daddy knows best.' We sometimes struggle to know what God's will is and consequently how we should pray. But living in submission to him should be our main priority. That may be hard to do, but it is not complicated.

'What does the Lord require of you?' To act justly and to love mercy and to walk humbly with your God' (Mic. 6:8).

We've all seen the drivers who consistently ignore the speed limits until they reach the cameras. Then the brakes go on. They drive impeccably for the few yards where they might be caught offending and then accelerate away.

We sometimes live our Christian lives as though we're being watched by speed cameras. When the eyes of the world, and particularly other believers, are on us, we can behave in a quite godly manner. We are more careful what we do and say than when we're alone. Paul illustrates this very human tendency when he instructs slaves to work hard even when the master isn't watching (Eph. 6:5-6).

Everyone does this to some extent. We present an acceptable front to the world, but behind closed doors our standards are not so high. Our families often see things in us we would rather our Christian brothers and sisters didn't know. And then there's what we allow our minds to dwell on, where even those closest to us cannot see. Even if our heart's desire is to live a holy life, the very fact that we have a private life and an inner world means that temptation within these realms is more difficult to resist.

Of course, we are deluding ourselves because the Lord sees everything we think or do, but for some reason, we conveniently forget about that at the point at which we dip our toe into the ocean of sin. Why is that?

The Lord Jesus said, 'If you love me you will obey what I command' (John 14:15). A corollary of that statement might be that our level of obedience to the Lord is determined by how much we love him. In other words, the more we love Jesus, the more determined we will be to resist temptation and stay away from sin.

We all know that feeling of conviction when we've missed the mark of God's perfect will. We know what it's like to have that black cloud between us and the Lord. It's not a comfortable place to be. Like the prodigal, we eventually come to our senses and repent.

Our sin doesn't just affect us; it affects the Lord. Whilst he is never surprised by what we do, it saddens our Father's heart that his children should go astray. But it is more awful than that. In one sense, it is as though we ourselves are hammering the nails into the hands and feet of Jesus. We are contributing to the sins which made his sacrificial suffering necessary.

It may be helpful to focus on the cross when we need to find the resources to resist temptation. But the crucifixion has already taken place, and whatever we do now does not add to the suffering of that dreadful day. Consequently it's easy to convince ourselves that one extra bit of sin doesn't really make a difference.

Throughout the Old Testament, when God's people turned away from him, he sent prophets who accused the nation of being an adulterous wife. Poor old Hosea even had to live prophetically, instructed by the Lord to take an unfaithful wife as a sign of the guilt of the people (Hos. 1:2).

We are part of the Bride of Christ and, like a husband, he is jealous for our affection. When we sin, he may be angry and disappointed. But he is also deeply hurt. When we fail to be obedient to him, we show a lack of love for him. Our devotion should be that of a bride. When we sin, we are looking to something or someone other than the Lord Jesus to satisfy our desires. Put bluntly, this is spiritual adultery. It is a shameful thing.

The power of the image of the unfaithful wife has been diminished in our culture. Adultery, divorce and remarriage, uncommitted relationships have all become unremarkable because they are so common. The breakdown of marriage is not only desperately sad for the individuals involved, it does damage to our understanding of our relationship with Jesus, the 'Lover of our souls' (Eph. 5:22-32).

But there is another powerful image which can reveal something more of the relationship between the Lord and his people. It is the image of God in us. When he created humanity, he said, 'Let us make man in our image.' Every individual since, though created unique, has been born with the image of God stamped in them like the lettering through a stick of seaside rock. Each one of us has been made to reflect that image in a way no other person can.

Since we are uniquely different and individual in character, personality, and spiritual qualities, we have a unique place in the Bride of Christ. Without us the Body, of which we are a part, would not be complete. Without us, there would be something missing from the beautiful Bride which the Father is preparing for his Son. Without us the, Bride would not be perfect.

In the Song of Songs, the lover says, 'You have ravished my heart, my sister my bride.' Dare we believe that the Lord says this of his Bride. Of course, because no human love affair can come close to that between Jesus and his people. This is why God was so jealous over Israel's unfaithfulness. Always the heart of God is to woo back his people to himself. He comes to you personally and lavishes his love on you. Why? Because you were uniquely created to be a part of his Bride, and there is a place in his heart that can only ever be touched by you.

There is, they say, a God-shaped hole in each of us that can only be filled with Jesus. I believe the uniqueness of every individual, whom God has created in his image, means that there is a you-shaped hole in the heart of God. When you give him your heart, when you live your life for him that hole is filled and he rejoices over you as a bridegroom rejoices over his bride (Isa. 62:5).

The more in love with the Lord Jesus we are, the greater will be our desire to remain faithful to him. No one who is truly in love could even contemplate adultery. The Lord's character is such that the more time we spend in his presence, the more deeply we will love him. Spending quality time alone with Jesus is not only good for our souls; it leads us on a journey away from sin and towards holiness of life. Time spent with him is never wasted.

In John 14, we see Jesus first promising to prepare a place for his disciples and to come back for them, then telling them he and the Father will come and make their home with them. That sounds to me like a passionate desire in the Lord's heart to be in our company. Your uniqueness delights God's heart. Your personal relationship with him does not have to conform to anybody's norms. All he wants is for you to be yourself with him and to allow him to conform you to his perfect image. This should inspire us to flee from sin.

Lot's wife gets a very bad press over her failure to respond correctly to the Word of God. It's not enough that she ended up as a pillar of salt. She is held up as an example to us of what happens if we're not obedient to God or if we're reluctant to leave our sin behind. If we're not careful, we can find ourselves taking a superior attitude as though we think we would never make such a fundamental mistake.

What we perhaps miss is how close Lot's wife was to getting it right. She was, after all, being obedient and running away from Sodom and the depravity there. How many of us can say that we actually run from sin? We all know the experience of the internal struggle we sometimes have to do the right thing when what we really want is to do the wrong thing.

Lot's wife was being far more committed than we often manage to be, but she still wasn't wholeheartedly obedient to the Lord. She had been told not to look back (Gen. 19:17), but she thought she could get away with a quick glimpse behind her as she ran. The result was devastating.

Was the Lord harsh on Lot's wife? Should he have punished her so severely for one little slip? Look more carefully at Verse 26. The woman's fate was not God's doing. She brought it upon herself. Her death was a direct consequence of her disobedience.

When, in our devotions, we hear the gentle voice of the Holy Spirit convicting us of sin, there is one route away from destruction, and that is rapid flight without looking back. Paul told the Corinthians to flee from sexual sin and idolatry (1 Cor. 6:18 and 10:14) and Timothy to flee from the evil desires of youth (2 Tim. 2:22).

There is no room for compromise in dealing with sin. Jesus said, 'If your right hand causes you to sin, cut it off' (Matt. 5:30). He knows more about conquering temptation than anyone, and we should heed his instruction.

Lot's wife should be a warning to us. Don't take the slightest chance with sin. The consequences could be devastating.

Scripture tells us there is a time for everything (Eccles. 3:1), and whilst Paul tells us to pray *continually* (1 Thess. 5:17), that is not quite the same as praying *continuously*. There is a time when prayer is an inappropriate response, and we see this in the way the Lord Jesus deals with temptation.

After his baptism, Jesus was led by the Holy Spirit to the place where he was to be tempted by Satan. As we read this passage, we perhaps interpret the account to mean that the devil waited forty days, until Jesus was weakened by fasting and hunger, before attempting the assault. But the parallel passages in Mark and Luke suggest that the temptation was going on throughout that time.

Fasting may weaken the body but, when accompanied by prayer, it strengthens the spirit. Knowing that it was the Lord's regular practice to find lonely places to pray, we can be sure that much of his time during these forty days would have been spent praying. The prayer and fasting were part of his preparation for dealing with the tempter.

Jesus taught his followers to pray, 'Lead us not into temptation.' In Gethsemane, he urged his disciples, 'Pray so that you will not fall into temptation.' If we are to triumph over temptation as the Lord did, then our prayer against it has to happen *before* we face the trial. If we wait until we are tempted, we are likely to fail for two important reasons. The first is that praying about a temptation focuses our mind on it at precisely the time we should be taking captive every thought and thinking about something else. Secondly, if we haven't prepared ourselves in prayer, we will not have settled the matter, in our own mind and spirit, of whether we actually do intend to be obedient to the Lord or if we might allow ourselves to be swayed. We open ourselves up to the possibility that the tempter may be able to convince us to do the wrong thing.

> The reason why many fail in battle is because they wait until the
> hour of battle. The reason why others succeed is because they have

gained their victory on their knees long before the battle came . . .
Anticipate your battles; fight them on your knees before temptation
comes, and you will always have victory. (RA Torrey)

At the point at which Jesus came face-to-face with Satan, he did not pray.
He simply quoted the scriptures at him. He took God's Word and wielded it
as a sword to counter the devil's attack. All the quotations he used came from
Deuteronomy. It seems he had been spending some of his time in the wilderness
studying and meditating on God's Law.

To deal with temptation, we need to pray for protection against it and for
the determination to stand firm before we face the temptation. If we have a
vulnerability in a particular area, we need to search the Bible to find specific
scriptures we can quote at the enemy when the time comes.

Exercise

Give some thought to whether there is an area of compromise in your life.
Are you struggling with a besetting sin, but unwilling to make the commitment
to run from it wholeheartedly and never return? Is your thought life pure
and holy, or do you allow images to grow in your mind that you would be
embarrassed for others to see? Are you praying against temptation or just
passively waiting for it to strike before you deal with it? Take some time, like
David, to let God search your heart (Ps. 139:23), and reveal the truth to you.
You might want to use the devotion entitled *No Compromise* at the back of
this book. Determine you are going to run, with everything you've got, away
from sin and, fixing your eyes on Jesus, complete the race marked out for you
(Heb. 12 : 1-2).

CHAPTER 12

Look Who's Talking

Brothers, I could not address you as spiritual but as worldly—mere
infants in Christ. I gave you milk, not solid food, for you were not
ready for it. Indeed you are still not ready. You are still worldly.

(1 Cor. 3:1-3)

When Paul wrote these words, he was addressing people who
were proud of their spiritual status. After all, didn't they have prophets among
them? Weren't they active in the use of spiritual gifts? Wasn't the Holy Spirit
working powerfully in their worship services?

But Paul points the finger at their spiritual *character* rather than their
spiritual *gifts* and says, 'You just don't get it. You're nothing more than babies,
and that's the way I have to treat you. You need to grow up before I can begin
to teach you anything meaningful.'

He describes them as worldly, literally 'fleshly.' Whereas they should be
seeing the world from the spiritual dimension, informed by the voice of the
Holy Spirit within them, they see only the evidence of their eyes. It is as though

they believe God has no genuine power in the world. They have not grasped the difference between fact and truth.

The fact was that Lazarus was dead and rotting in the grave with no hope of another day of life. The truth was that it was always the intention of the Lord Jesus to raise him from the dead and to bring glory to God through the miracle (John 11-12).

The fact was that the people on the hillside were hungry, and there wasn't enough food to go around. The truth was that Jesus was able to multiply the packed lunch given to him by a child so that everyone was well fed (Mark 6:30-44).

The fact was that the storm was raging so violently that the little fishing boat could capsize at any moment. The truth was that Jesus had said they *were* going to the other side of the lake (Mark 4:35-41).

Jesus said, 'You shall know the truth and the truth shall set you free' (John 8:32). Focusing on facts bind us, seeing the truth liberates us. Materialism deals in facts and dulls the mind into thinking that there is no such thing as ultimate truth. It tempts us to focus on what we can see and touch. It makes wealth and external beauty attractive and causes us to rage against people who upset our chances of achieving our goals. We feel helpless before the might of the State or the bully at work. We see wars and famines around the world and feel powerless. We look at our meager income and the rate of inflation and fear for the well-being of our family.

Innumerable times during his earthly ministry, the Lord said, 'I tell you the truth.' He is the only reliable source of truth. If we are to know the truth, we need to be completely steeped in his Word, in scripture. This will enable us to hear the voice of the Holy Spirit and get a divine perspective on the world around us.

Back in our original passage, Paul uses a word to describe the Corinthians which is most illuminating in its original Greek form. That word 'infants' literally means 'non-speakers', in other words, those who haven't learnt how to talk yet. This was how Paul knew they were immature spiritually—by the way they talked. Their words came from thoughts dictated to by the world, by what they experienced through their flesh. They talked about facts as though facts were the only reality. Consequently there was jealousy and quarrelling. Their spirit, on the other hand, was so underdeveloped that it had no voice. It was not informing their thinking or their actions.

There is always a bigger picture, always a spiritual dimension to what is going on in the material world. The book of Revelation partially draws back the curtain so that we can momentarily see the spiritual warfare which undergirds the events of the material world. And the overall message of Revelation is that God always wins. Whatever is going on in our personal lives or the world around us, God is at work to fulfill his divine purposes. The spiritually mature focus on this truth rather than on the facts which the unspiritual lament.

We all have a need for our spirits to grow. We all should be striving for spiritual maturity. The way to do this is to actively cultivate our spiritual lives and not just to wait for God to bring about our growth. Bible reading, fellowship with more mature believers, and spending time in the presence of the Lord Jesus in prayer and worship are key to this process. When we see our lives from a spiritual dimension, we will be more able to cooperate with the Lord in his work to make us his Bride.

I know a millionaire who says that if you want to be successful, you should duplicate what successful people do. For him, in his quest after material success, this means reading the newspapers successful people read, listening to talks by successful people, putting in the kind of hours they do. I have to say that I cannot argue with him—his method reaps the reward he's after: fast cars, luxury home, holidays all over the world. Others who want that kind of life can learn a lot from him, and he is helping them to find similar levels of success—he has disciples. If we want to become more spiritually 'successful', then we need to be disciples, modeling ourselves on others who have gone before and in particular on the Lord Jesus.

Spiritual maturity is inextricably tied up with prayer. It is impossible to become spiritually mature without spending time in the presence of God and seeking for him to open our eyes and transform us.

Exercise

God promises blessings for people of character. This is summed up beautifully in the passage that has become known as the Beatitudes (Matt. 5:3-10). Turn to *The Beatitudes* in the Devotions section at the back of this book and pray through it as described there.

CHAPTER 13

What Is Worship?

Worship is first and foremost for His benefit, not ours, though it is marvelous to discover that in giving Him pleasure, we ourselves enter into what can become our richest and most wholesome experience in life.

(Graham Kendrick)

In the past, I've heard several people comment that they find it difficult to worship within the context of their personal devotions.

As for me, I'm in agreement with Graham Kendrick, so I want us to spend some time thinking about what worship is and make some practical suggestions, which I hope will be helpful.

I am absolutely convinced that part of the problem people have with personal worship is that they get it mixed up with adoration. The two are not the same for one very important reason. Adoration requires the involvement of emotion, but worship does not. I might say that I adore my children, and you would understand that I mean I have deep feelings of love towards them. But I do not worship them.

Perhaps the best way to understand worship is to look at those passages of scripture which describe the worship of heaven. One example is Revelation 5:6-14. It is the vision of the Lamb and the scroll. The living creatures and the elders fall before the throne in worship and begin by saying, 'You are worthy.'

Our word *worship* comes from the Old English word *woerthscipe*, which literally means to tell someone their worth. This is exactly what we see the worshippers doing in this passage in Revelation. They tell the Lord that he is worthy because . . . he was slain, he bought men for God through his blood, he has created a kingdom of priests. All of these are statements of fact. There is little emotional content here.

When we come to personal worship, the place to start is with telling God facts about himself. In doing this, we are acknowledging to him, before all the powers of the spiritual realm, and to ourselves, that we recognise he truly is God. We are reminded of his nature and his character. This takes a lot of pressure off us. We don't have to worry about how we feel or whether we're worthy to come into his presence. We simply worship because he is worthy to receive our worship, not because we feel like it. In fact, if we wait until we do feel like it, we may never enter into worship at all.

I want to emphasise that there is no need for any emotional content at the very beginning of worship. I do not have to say, 'I love you because you are the Prince of Peace.' I can simply say, 'You are the Prince of Peace.' It is a statement of fact, it is fundamentally true, it is what scripture tells me the Lord is like, and to tell him so is worship even if the concept does not initially excite me. Worship is something we have to discipline ourselves to do.

However, my experience of this kind of worship is that it immeasurably enhances my devotional times. Firstly, acknowledging and recognising who God is gets my perspective right. When we are privileged to call him our Father and to come to him as little children, it is all too easy to become overly casual with God and to forget how holy and awesome he is. Secondly, when I worship in this way, I find it inspires me to adoration. Where I might not have been feeling much love towards God when I started, the emotions well up inside of me as I focus on his character and nature. Thirdly, the Lord often responds to this kind of worship by making his felt presence a reality. If I am feeling far from God, a simple decision to offer worship can be all that is required to restore a sense of fellowship with him. Fourthly, it is often in these times of worship that the Lord puts his finger on something in my life that needs to change, especially if my focus has been on his holiness.

So, how do we actually do this thing called worship? Here are some suggestions.

For many people, the easiest place to begin is with singing. We find this simple because we are used to doing it in church. Get a hymn book and look for songs and hymns that are truly worshipful and speak directly to God (you'd be surprised how many things we sing are really only addressed to ourselves or other people and not to the Lord). In your quiet time, you can read the words or sing them.

You can also look through scripture for statements about who God is and what he's like and simply repeat them back to him. The Psalms and Isaiah are particularly good sources for this when you are just starting. But you could keep a notepad and record any phrases you come across in your daily readings which you can use in your worship times.

Use your own life as a source for worshipful thoughts. How have you seen God work in your life in the past? What does that show about his nature? That he is faithful, long suffering, kind, tender, powerful, your healer, your comforter, your best friend? Tell him that you have seen that these things are true from your own experience.

As we have said before, some people find that particular postures in prayer enhance worship. I tend simply to follow my heart and do what feels appropriate at the time, but if I am aware that I am struggling to focus on God in worship, I find kneeling or *bowing down*, in what might be described as the Muslim posture, can be helpful. But the most important thing is attitude of heart rather than our physical position. Let us take another biblical example.

> And Mary said, 'My soul glorifies the Lord and my spirit rejoices in
> God my Saviour.' (Luke 1:46-47)

In the best Hebrew tradition, Mary's response to a divine encounter is a song of praise. This is such a well-known passage, included in the liturgy of some denominational churches and a familiar part of Christmas celebrations, that it is all too easy to rush through it without thinking about its content. But the first few phrases can help us to understand something about the nature of worship when we take them in the context of the Christian constitution—how we are made.

In 1 Thessalonians 5:23, Paul blesses those he is writing to by saying, 'May your whole spirit, soul and body be kept blameless.' This verse clarifies what is hinted at elsewhere in scripture that we are tripartite beings. There are three elements to our nature. We have no difficulty understanding the concept of *body*, but there is sometimes confusion around the meanings of *soul* and *spirit*, both of which are used at the beginning of Mary's hymn of praise. The words are often used interchangeably by Christians, but this is incorrect and leads to all kinds of confusion and sometimes to a limitation in our understanding of worship.

In fact, the soul consists of the mind, will, and emotions whereas the spirit is that part of us which communicates with God. As one preacher puts it, 'I am a spirit, I have a soul and I live in a body.' The Lord Jesus taught us that those who worship God must do so in spirit and in truth (John 4:24). He did not say this because worship is a purely spiritual activity, but to emphasise that true worship goes beyond what is going on in our body and soul. Mary's song helps us to understand this.

First, the blindingly obvious—Mary's words were spoken. When we sing songs of worship, we use our bodies. We inflate our lungs with air which, when released, passes over our vocal cords to produce the sound shaped by our mouths. Often we use other parts of our body in worship too. We may kneel down, raise our hands, or close our eyes.

The soul is also engaged when we worship. We use our will to decide to worship, our mind comprehends the words we use and our emotions are often also involved—we are thrilled by a rousing hymn, inspired to love and perhaps even moved to tears by more devotional songs.

This is where we can slip into thinking that we are worshipping in spirit when, in reality, our spirit has not yet been engaged. Even secular music often arouses an emotional response in people, but that is not the same as making a spiritual connection with God.

So what is spiritual worship?

> Prayer is occupation with my needs, praise is occupation with my blessings, but worship is occupation with God Himself. (Leonard Ravenhill)

While Mary says that her soul 'glorifies the Lord', she states that her spirit 'rejoices *in* God'. Any soul can glorify God by making a decision of the will to do so. A Buddhist or Hindu could stand and read aloud passages of the Bible which speak about how wonderful our God is. This would bring glory to him even though the reader was making no spiritual connection. He or she might even find the words and concepts emotionally stirring. But they will not be worshipping.

Mary, however, was making a spiritual connection. That little word, 'in' is not there simply because of the grammatical structure of the sentence. It shows us that there is communion between God and the worshipper. This goes beyond mind, will, and emotion to revelation. In the words of songwriter Matt Redman, *worship starts with seeing You.*

It is impossible to adequately describe spiritual experiences. Unless someone has had an encounter with God, they cannot understand. Because a spiritual experience often evokes an emotional response, such as love or joy, or even a physical response, weeping or trembling for example, it may sometimes be explained in the language of body and soul. This can lead to some people believing that if they have an emotional response they are worshipping.

One of my favourite passages is Luke 7:36-50. Here the sinful woman expresses worship physically, wetting Jesus's feet with her tears drying them with her hair and then pouring perfume on them. The tears show that her soul is also involved as she is overwhelmed with emotion. The Lord tells the Pharisee who complained about her behaviour, 'She loved much.' He tells the woman, Your sins are forgiven and 'Your faith has saved you.' This is the nub of the matter. Worship in spirit is a matter of faith, the unavoidable response of the sinner who recognises the extent of their own depravity, and the divine love that brings salvation. This is the revelation Mary also had when she said, 'My spirit rejoices *in* God my Saviour.'

Five times in Ephesians, Paul uses the phrase, 'heavenly realms' to describe the spiritual dimension which is outside time and space. This is the place where we connect with God and worship him. It is where we are seated with Christ (Eph. 2:6) and the one place we can experience the totality of what it means to be human because our entire being (body, soul, *and* spirit) can be active in worship.

Exercise

Make a list of twenty statements from scripture which describe the nature and character of the Lord. Write them down in the form, 'You are . . .' Use some of them at the beginning of each prayer time over the next few days. Don't just rush through them, but think about the meaning and implications of each one and try to expand on them in your own words.

CHAPTER 14

Take Your Time

The hours I spent communing with the Lord Jesus catapulted me
into a whole new dimension of joy in the Lord. Those hours—and
many hours since—have ushered me into the deep recesses of my
Saviour's heart.

(Joni Eareckson Tada)

few years ago, finding myself with just fifteen minutes to prepare
a sermon, I decided to fall back on the subject of prayer. One of the passages I
referred to was Matthew 6:36-45. The Lord Jesus is praying in Gethsemane and
seeking the support of his disciples who are woefully lacking in their prayers. At
the heart of this passage is the Lord's question, 'Couldn't you even watch with me
for one hour?' An hour of prayer seems a huge leap from the paltry ten minutes of
prayer I mentioned in an earlier chapter. Most people would baulk at the idea.

There are probably three main reasons why the thought of praying for an
hour is just too much for many Christians.

The first is time. People don't know where in their daily schedule they
are going to find an extra hour for anything. But I've discovered something

amazing. Our heavenly Father blesses everyone with the same number of hours in the day—twenty-four. Highly productive people such as politicians and businessmen only have the same amount of time available to them as we do each day. It's just that some people use their time more wisely than others. If you had to find an extra hour in the day to cope with some emergency, you could find it. Here are some ideas for how to find that extra hour: give up an hour of TV each day, get up an hour earlier, reassess the time you spend on various chores—does the car really need washing every week?

The second reason is found in past experience. Many people don't have a positive experience of prayer. Prayer, when it's functioning properly, is an intimate relationship between the believer and their Lord. As we have already said, the communication is supposed to be two-way. It's not simply about taking our requests to God, it's also about hearing him speak to us and, as Joni Eareckson Tada intimates, enjoying his company. Why is it that some Christians don't have this fulfilling experience in prayer? It's quite simple. It takes time to develop a relationship, and it cannot be done simply by rushing into the throne room with our petitions and then rushing out again. God reserves the reward of the experience of his presence to those who are willing to 'waste' time in the prayer closet.

But the final, and perhaps most honest, explanation is that many people just don't know what on earth they are going to do in prayer for a whole hour. It's like contemplating a marathon when you can barely run to catch the bus. However, if you can pray for five minutes, you *can* pray for an hour. It is simply a matter of segmenting the time into 'bite-sized chunks' and focusing on a different aspect of prayer for each—confession, worship, thanksgiving, intercession, supplication, and so on. So far, we have focused primarily on worship and enjoying the presence of God. Later in this book, I want to explore different aspects of prayer in more detail and see how we will gain a growing desire to spend longer in prayer each day. For now, I want to set before you a grand vista of the potential in your own prayer life as it grows. There is nothing special about people who pray for an hour—you can do it too.

We've considered the idea of church leaders spending a mere ten minutes a day in prayer and the concept of consecrating an hour each day for prayer. But is time the most important thing? Certainly, it's not the case that God answers lengthy prayers more willingly than short ones. I personally have found that single word prayers such as '*help*'! can be particularly effective. We must not get hung up on counting the minutes we spend on our knees. What really matters is effectiveness, though what we might consider effective prayer is not necessarily what God considers effective.

I find the example of Abraham fascinating, and I want us to look briefly at one of his encounters with God in prayer which is recorded in Genesis 18:20-33. Abraham was pleading with God for the lives of the people of Sodom. He stood before God and repeatedly asked him to spare Sodom for the sake of any righteous people living there—*will You also destroy the righteous with the wicked?* Abraham seemed to be negotiating with God as he repeated his request time and again, until the Lord agreed he would not destroy Sodom for the sake of ten righteous people. The boldness of Abraham is worthy of consideration, but what I find most fascinating about this passage is that it was not Abraham who ended the conversation. It was God (verse 33). 'When the Lord had finished speaking with Abraham, He left, and Abraham returned home.' Only when God had finished with Abraham did Abraham leave the place of prayer.

How many of us can say that that is how we pray? Do we pray until we're done or until God is done? Imagine walking out of a conversation with your boss, your best friend, or your spouse just because you've said all you wanted to say but leaving them wanting to say more. You wouldn't do it. Why would you do it with God?

So the answer to the question 'how long should I pray?' is not a specific length of time. We should pray until the Lord has finished his dealings with us. There are no gold stars for praying for two hours if all God has to say to us today is, 'Go and tell your neighbour about me.' Equally, we must be wary of rushing away from the Lord's presence when he has more for us.

In our culture, it is extremely hard to find space to give the Lord an open-ended amount of time. We have responsibilities with work and family that the Lord has given us and which should not be neglected. On most days, we will be limited with our time. The Lord knows this and will honour us for giving the time we have. But we *can* find space sometimes to give extended time to the Lord and the blessings which will flow from that are inexpressible.

Let's look at an example of someone who decided to wait as long as it took.

> Then the disciples went back to their homes, but Mary (Magdalene) stood . . . (John 20:10-11)

We all have different expectations and experiences of our encounters with the Lord Jesus. John's Gospel shows us the reactions of three individuals when they discover the empty tomb which can teach us something about our prayer lives.

Peter behaves true to form. When he hears the tomb is empty, he rushes to the scene to see what is going on. He doesn't get there first but, once he's seen the proof that what he was told is true, he's off home again. It's hard to see that this experience does anything more than cause puzzlement. His time at the tomb does not answer any questions for him.

John, on the other hand, gets there first and has longer to take in what's going on. He, we are told, sees and believes. His time at the tomb takes him beyond the plain facts which Peter saw and into the realm of faith before he, too, goes home.

Mary's experience, however, is the most powerful. The word, *stood*, could just as well have been translated to *waited* as it is elsewhere in John's Gospel. Unlike the men, she doesn't go straight home; she remains there weeping. She doesn't understand what's going on, but this emotional woman seems to want simply to be as close to Jesus as possible and that, for her, means staying at the last place where she knows he was.

Three amazing things happen. First she sees two angels, a remarkable enough experience on its own. Then she has the single most privileged encounter in history for she is the first to meet the risen Lord himself. Finally she receives the commission from Jesus to go and tell the other disciples. She is the first person to preach the resurrection of Christ. She is the one to report, 'I have seen the Lord!'

In our personal devotions, we can be like Peter, dashing in and out of our prayer time without any encounter with Jesus. Or we can be like John, with a degree of discernment which enhances our spiritual experience.

Or we can be like Mary Magdalene, someone who can be totally themselves with Jesus, who waits around in the prayer closet until he arrives with his own unique love and compassion, meeting every need, and commissioning for service.

The question is, are you prepared to 'waste time' hanging around, waiting for Jesus?

Exercise

Make a space in your diary in the coming week when you can give the Lord an open-ended time. Begin that time by worshipping him with the words of Psalm 8. Ask him to direct your prayers and then pray about whatever comes to mind. When you have done this, sit quietly, listening for his voice in your heart. Respond in whatever way seems appropriate. Rest until you feel ready to leave your sacred space.

If finding an available time slot for this is difficult, consider trying one of the options many saints have used as they have emulated the prayer life of the Lord Jesus—use the night hours for prayer. There is no need to commit yourself to an entire night of prayer, but you can decide to pray into the night until you're done.

CHAPTER 15

Structuring Your Time

Our primary task is not to calculate how many verses of Scripture we read or how many minutes we spend in prayer. Our task is to use these activities to create opportunities for God to work. Then what happens is up to Him.

(John Ortberg)

I don't really like advising people how to structure their time with God. Just as every marriage is different, so is every relationship between the believer and their Lord. What works for one Christian in their devotional time won't work for someone else. I also believe that flexibility is key. Perhaps it's because I'm the kind of person who gets bored with always taking the same route to the supermarket, but I find variety to be essential. But there are those who like to take the same route and have a favourite parking spot. So if you're one of those, or you're very new to all of this, we should perhaps, having worked through some introductory exercises, lay down some guidelines so that no one is left floundering.

First though, let's deal with some terminology. Many use the phrase 'Quiet Time' to describe the time they set aside especially to spend with God each day.

It seems to have been first used in this context by an American evangelist Frank Buchman (1878-1961). Its popularity of usage is probably due to its simplicity and the fact that it sounds quite friendly. In fact, the idea of a quiet time was incorporated into the twelve-step programme of Alcoholics Anonymous! Other terms used include devotions, prayer time, and time with God. They all mean pretty much the same, but quiet time slips off the tongue most easily. So what should we include in our quiet time?

We have discussed worship a great deal because it is the foundation of our relationship with God. Without worship, we will not be in tune with the voice of the Holy Spirit speaking through his Word, prompting us in how to pray and gently convicting us of sin.

> It is because of the hasty and superficial conversation with God that
> the sense of sin is so weak and that no motives have power to help
> you to hate and flee from sin as you should. (AW Tozer)

Beginning a structured quiet time with worship in some form is essential, whether that be using our own words or those of a psalm, hymn, or spiritual song.

Worship has the tendency to flow in two possible directions. One, as indicated by Tozer, is conviction of sin, confession, repentance, and receiving forgiveness. We need to be wary of spending too much time digging around looking for every tiny thing that might possibly constitute sin. It is the Holy Spirit's job to convict us of sin (John 16:7-8). Our role is to ask *him* to search our hearts (Ps. 139:23-24) and respond to what he shows us.

The other possible direction is thanksgiving. Often as we worship, we are reminded of things God has done for us, either the routine things such as health and home or those specific answers to prayers we have prayed. Thanksgiving is essential as it keeps our attitude towards God in the right perspective. He is a generous God, and the more we recognise his generosity, the more trusting we will be and the more we will want to pray. It will also be the case that we will be more receptive when the answer to our prayers is 'no'. It is easier to accept that kind of answer from someone we know gives us blessings because we can trust there is a good reason for him withholding what we have asked for.

There will be more to thank God for when we are actually asking him for things. I want to talk more about this business of intercession and supplication later. For now, I simply want to say that it is an important part of a quiet time. Some people, when they first start taking prayer seriously, feel overwhelmed by all the things and people they could be praying for. Let me liberate you. God does not expect you to pray for everything. What he expects is that you pray for the things that are on your heart. As we have said before, God gives us the desires of our hearts, so listen to the prompting of the Holy Spirit about what you should be praying for. If each individual Christian would take that responsibility seriously, then every person's needs would be covered in prayer.

> Jesus Christ carries on intercession for us in heaven; the Holy Ghost carries on intercession in us on earth; and we the saints have to carry on intercession for all men. (Oswald Chambers)

The final element of a quiet time, though not necessarily to be held back to the end, is Bible reading. I want to make a very clear distinction here between Bible *study* and *devotional* Bible reading because the two are not the same.

Bible study is important to a balanced Christian life. It consists of taking a passage of scripture and finding out the background of the passage, its setting, what the language actually means, and so on, usually with the help of some kind of written guide. It is essential to understanding God and his ways. Some people include this kind of study in their quiet time, but it is quite time-consuming if done properly, and for most of us it is better to set aside a separate time to do Bible study.

For all of us, though, devotional reading is vital. You do need some kind of system. Dipping into favourite passages or simply opening the Bible at random will not do. Some people like to use booklets of dated notes which are usually sermonettes on a verse or short passage of scripture. This kind of thing may have its place when you are starting out, but it is not really an adequate substitute for listening to God yourself. For a start, the passage is being interpreted to you by another human being rather than God himself. Secondly, thousands of people are reading the same passage and comments on the same day as you—is God's Word to each of these individual people really exactly the same on the same day? It is much better to learn to recognise the sound of his voice for yourself, rather than rely on someone else hearing it for you.

So plan your own reading scheme. There are plenty of guides out there which will give you a format for reading the whole Bible in three years or twelve months, without lots of commentary, which you might use as a basis. There are now lots of plans freely available on the Internet too. But remember that the goal is not to see how quickly you can get through it. Rather, the aim is to learn to hear God's voice through his Word so you can simply decide for yourself how to do it. But do try to be systematic, or there will be whole chunks of the Bible which you may never read—most people don't go into Leviticus or Chronicles expecting to be thrilled by what they read. Starting at Genesis and working through to Revelation might not be the best plan. You could perhaps start with the Gospels or the Psalms.

Take a few moments before you start reading to focus on the Lord and ask him to speak to you through your reading. Turn to the passage and start reading. Your aim is not to complete a certain number of verses but to hear God's voice. So if something you read seems to have meaning for you, stop and think about it. Mull it over; ask God to help you understand what he wants you to get from it. Write down what you think he might be saying; look up other passages which might be relevant (good Bibles will have cross references in the margin), respond to God, thank him for speaking to you. Later in the day, remind yourself of what you have read and what God seemed to be saying. In your next quiet time, continue reading from where you left off in the previous one.

It's worth offering a comment on versions of the Bible. The key thing is to get one you understand. Many people love the Authorised Version. As I write, we are celebrating its four hundredth anniversary. It was an excellent translation in its day, but like the plays of Shakespeare which come from around the same era, you really need to be taught about the language to understand it properly. If you've been brought up with it and are comfortable with it, by all means use it. Otherwise get a modern translation. A good Christian bookshop will be able to advise you.

Exercise

Work through the Sample quiet time in the Devotions section. See if it is a structure that works for you. Don't worry if it doesn't—modify it!

CHAPTER 16

Good Morning Lord

In the morning, O Lord, you hear my voice.

(Psalm 5:3)

I wonder what your first thought is on waking. As I once heard someone comment, do you find yourself saying, 'Good morning, Lord,' or is it more a case of, 'good Lord! Morning.' Are you fumbling for the alarm clock wishing you'd gone to bed an hour earlier the night before? Do you have an immediate sinking feeling as you realise the challenges that are ahead of you? Or are you one of those people who gets excited by the prospect of a new day and can't wait to leap out of bed and get going? How long is it before the Lord enters your thoughts?

We are all different—fearfully and wonderfully made, to use the psalmist's words (Ps. 139:14). As we have said before, we're at our most alert at different times of the day—some in the morning, some in the afternoon, some in the evening. If at all possible we should give our best time to the Lord for our personal devotions. The early part of the day suits many people very well but others find they cannot concentrate sufficiently until later.

Either way though, whatever our own personal internal clock is like, if we are aiming to live for, and walk with, the Lord Jesus throughout the day, the sooner he enters our thoughts, the better. A friend of mine commented to his Sunday School class that it is a good practice to say, 'good morning, Lord' right at the beginning of the day, even if you don't catch up with him properly until later in the day. But how do you do that? How do you train your mind so that your very first thought is of God, rather than getting half way through the morning before you even remember him?

I have stumbled across one way of doing this. It may not suit everyone but it works for me. I have found that when I listen to music my mind tends to carry on playing it even when I stop listening. If I have a worship CD on in the car when I go shopping, the same song that was playing on the stereo when I got out of the car in the supermarket car park is playing in my head when I return to the car and switch it on again. In fact, if I pay attention, that song has been buzzing round my head all the time I was shopping, even though I may have been doing mental arithmetic all the time to make sure I don't go over budget.

I have discovered that if I listen to enough music during the day there is always a worship song playing in the back of my mind. I've even found that sleep doesn't switch off my internal stereo. If I've been listening to Christian music or singing towards the end of the day, there is often a hymn of praise already playing in my head when I wake up. As I emerge from sleep my soul is already singing to the Lord.

Our minds like to wander off on their own like inquisitive children so they need to be disciplined to set themselves on God. Because of this we have to be careful to give them the right kind of input. I've used the example of worship songs, but I believe that taking time every day to focus on scripture or on prayer can be equally effective. The key is to decide not to allow your mind to become idle and distracted, but to use as much of its spare capacity as possible to focus on the Lord.

We take captive every thought to make it obedient to Christ.

(2 Corinthians 10:5)

We cannot afford to let our minds wander even on to apparently safe byways. Our whole lives need to be submitted to Christ. This has additional benefits.

You will keep in perfect peace those whose minds are steadfast, because they trust in you.

(Isaiah 26:3)

Not only will a disciplined mind be focused enough to be set on God from the moment we wake in the mornings, it will also reap untold rewards in terms of peace. When our minds are steadfast, to use Isaiah's word, fixed on the things of God, then nothing can disturb our trust in him. If we have set our minds on God from the very start of the day we can have peace throughout the following 24 hours because we have a heavenly perspective rather than an earthly one.

Love the Lord your God with all your heart and with all your soul and with all your mind and with all your strength.

(Mark 12:30)

We have to make the decision that we are going to love the Lord with all of our minds including in those first conscious moments of the day. It will not happen by accident, it takes an act of the will to obey the command of Jesus in Mark 12, to offer him our love in this way.

Exercise

When you go to bed tonight ask the Lord to give you a peaceful night. Then sing (preferably in your head, especially if you share your sleeping quarters with someone else!) a favourite hymn or spiritual song. In case you forget overnight, write down what it is. Tomorrow morning begin your day with the same song. It may not happen that you immediately have the experience of waking with a song in your heart. As with so many things in the Christian life it can take repeated practice before it bears the fruit. So be prepared to persist in this until your first thoughts in the morning are of the Lord.

Of course we can also make use of modern technology. If your mobile phone has a function which allows you to set a music track as an alarm, why not download a worship song to wake you up in the morning. You could even consider getting an mp3 version of someone reading the Bible and set that as your alarm. There are several versions available.

CHAPTER 17

Confession

If we claim to be without sin, we deceive ourselves and the truth is
not in us. If we confess our sins, he is faithful and just and will forgive
us our sins and purify us from all unrighteousness.

(1 John 1:8-9)

The word *confess* simply means *to acknowledge* or *to declare*. Within the
context of Christian faith, it has been adopted to cover a number of different
concepts. The one I want us to look at in this chapter, within the subject of
prayer, is admission of guilt.

The traditional version of the Lord's prayer includes the phrase, 'forgive us
our trespasses,' so we can see that seeking forgiveness from God is a vital part
of prayer. But this word *trespasses* is not one that is in common usage today so
it benefits from some explanation. Modern versions of this prayer use *debts* or
sins, two words which have quite different connotations. Interestingly, the two
passages in the Gospels which contain the Lord's prayer have different Greek
words underlying the English too.

Here we are going to take a slight diversion into New Testament Greek so we can understand a little more about confession and forgiveness.

In Luke 11:4, the Greek word used is *hamartias* which is the usual word for sin which implies making an error or missing the mark, in other words, falling short of perfection. We would like to define sin as being when we deliberately do something wrong. That would let us off a lot of hooks. We could think of ourselves as good if we only made minor mistakes which didn't really hurt anyone. But the Bible won't allow for this kind of self-delusion—for all have sinned and fall short of the glory of God (Rom. 3:23).

James tells us that whoever breaks just one small point of the law is guilty of breaking all of it (Jas. 2:10). Unlike current legal systems which have different documents defining what is and isn't legal in different aspects life, the Israelites were given one single master document to cover their whole legal system. We have different Acts of Parliament for road traffic offences, burglary, murder, education, and so on. The Israelites had Deuteronomy. We think of breaking only certain laws and not others as making us somehow less guilty. God's standard is different. While there are different punishments for different types of crime, all lawbreakers are equally guilty. I don't want to get stuck in too much theology here—a whole book could be devoted to the subject. Suffice it to say that it is not simply individual sins that need to be confessed but our sinful nature, our inability to keep the entirety of God's law.

In Matthew 6:12, the Greek word translated debts is *opselemata* from a root, meaning a debt or obligation. In our materialistic world, we are all too familiar with the concept of financial debt and being obliged to repay what we owe. The only way out of debt is to pay it off or to legally declare oneself bankrupt. When we ask God to forgive our debts, we are declaring our moral bankruptcy before him and acknowledging there is nothing we can do to make ourselves righteous. All we can do is ask that God no longer counts our debt against us. We are asking for a legally binding accounting contract which will no longer demand what we owe.

Now all of this is important because it points us back to the heart of the Gospel which is that God is just and cannot accept us in our sin. God will not simply write off the debt as some people believe. The price has to be paid by someone, and that someone is the Lord Jesus Christ who paid it on the cross at Calvary. However, you have to accept that payment for yourself. It's not automatic. People today are being told to invite Jesus into their heart. This is not in the Bible. On the contrary, we are told in scripture to 'repent, then, and turn to God, so that your sins may be wiped out' (Acts 3:19). That word repent literally means to turn around through 180 degrees and go the other way. In the Christian context, it means to turn away from living your life your way and do the complete opposite, living God's way. That means submitting our own ideas to God's Word—if I disagree with the Book, I'm the one who needs to change.

It is not enough to confess what we have done wrong or even to confess that we have an inherently sinful nature. Confession on its own is simply a statement of fact. It amazes me how many people with short tempers are actually proud of the fact. They confess it freely with no sense that they need to repent and behave differently. All that confession does is warn people there might be trouble. God wants us to be remorseful and repentant. He is looking for a change of heart and for us to *produce fruit in keeping with repentance* (Matt. 3:8).

In times of revival, when the church begins to grow at unprecedented rates and large numbers of people are being converted (changed), there is *always* a great deal of genuine repentance usually with tears of remorse. There may be signs and wonders too, but these are secondary and repentance and confession are the true marks of revival, just as they are the true marks of Christian conversion.

Not only are these the marks of conversion, they will continue to be an ongoing part of a Christian's prayer life. The Christian's desire is to be pure-hearted before God. This is exemplified by David's words.

Search me, O God, and know my heart;

Test me and know my anxious thoughts.

See if there is any offensive way in me,

And lead me in the way everlasting. (Ps. 139:23-24)

Repentance becomes an inherent part of a Christian lifestyle, not out of duty, but out of love for the Saviour who sacrificed himself.

The flip side of the confession and repentance coin is forgiveness. There seems to be something built into the human psyche which recognises that if we do something wrong, we deserve punishment and that we have to pay in some way. The passage at the beginning of this chapter reminds us that God's currency includes faithfulness and justice. Justice is appeased by the death of Christ, and God's faithfulness will not allow him to do anything other than to adhere to that justice. So we can be confident that when we come and confess with a repentant attitude, we will be forgiven. We should never allow ourselves to think that we also need to be punished. There is one sacrifice for atonement. There is no need for penance or metaphorical sackcloth and ashes, being gloomy and depressed. Forgiveness needs to be accepted fully so that we are available to God for what he wants to do in and through us.

That is not to say that restitution should not be made if we have offended against a person. There are detailed laws in the Old Testament about restitution, and Jesus taught that the moment we realise our brother has something against us, we should go and sort it out (Matt. 5:23-26). If what you have done has caused someone else to lose out, you need to put it right.

Nor is it a case that being forgiven by God means that you get away with the consequences. There may be major implications to be faced up to. God is not going to remove the points from your driving licence after you've been found guilty of dangerous driving, neither is he going to miraculously heal the disease which resulted from an unholy sexual relationship. But if you do repent and cast yourself on him, he will get you through the resulting problems, and you will learn valuable lessons, not simply about getting yourself in a mess, but also about the love and faithfulness of God.

Exercise

Take some time to be still before God and ask him to examine your heart as David did. If you are not sure whether you have ever truly confessed your sinful nature, repented of the sin of going your own way rather than God's and received forgiveness, you might like to use the Prayer of Repentance in the Devotions section.

CHAPTER 18

God Keeps His Word

Here is one of the greatest secrets of prevailing prayer: to study the Word to find what God's will is as revealed there in the promises, and then simply take these promises and spread them out before God in prayer with the absolutely unwavering expectation that He will do what He has promised in His Word.

(RA Torrey)

One of the strategies my children use to get what they want (or need) is to remind me of what I've said. It can be extremely frustrating to get to 4:30 on a Saturday afternoon and be told, 'You said you would take me to the shop today so that I can spend my pocket money.' What can I do? I'd forgotten I'd made that promise until he reminded me. If I try to get out of it, I will be saying to my son that he can't always trust me. Our relationship will be damaged because he is looking forward to the trip and I will have failed him. So I tell him he'd better get his shoes on quickly!

I agree to go partly because, if I don't, he will pester me incessantly. But I agree mainly because I had made a promise to him, and I try to do all I can to keep my word to my children.

God is like this too. There are differences, He doesn't forget the promises he has made, and he isn't frustrated when we remind him about them at the last minute. On the contrary, he is waiting to hear us take the promises from scripture, remind him of them in prayer, and call upon him to fulfill them. It really is very simple; all you have to do is be diligent in reading scripture so that you know what God's promises are and then start to use them in your prayers. Here is a very simple example.

I have had to deal with some particular interpersonal issues recently. I have needed the right words for the right time and have needed to know when to speak up and when to remain silent. My greatest need has been wisdom. Now I know that in the Bible. It says:

> If any of you lacks wisdom, he should ask God, who gives generously to all without finding fault, and it will be given to him. (James 1:5)

So I have prayed something like this:

> *Lord, you know the situation I am in. I don't want to get this wrong and cause offence. Your word says that you give wisdom to those who ask so I am asking you for wisdom to know what to say and when to say it.*

There have been times when I have wondered how I was going to feed the family, and I have prayed:

> *Lord, you are my Shepherd and Psalm 23 says that because you are my Shepherd I shall not be in want. Please keep your promise and provide for my family.*

When I have been unable to sleep, I have reminded him that his word says that he gives sleep to his beloved (Ps. 127:2); when I have been devastated by a loss, I have reminded him that he binds up the broken hearted (Isa. 61:1); in praying for a bereaved friend, I call on him to reveal himself to her as her husband (Isa. 54:5).

It is not disrespectful to God to be very bold in approaching him in this way. I often find myself saying, 'Lord, I want to remind you that your word says...' It is not that I think he has forgotten what he has promised, it is simply that I am reminding myself that he has made a promise and that promise is firm. In fact, a lack of boldness is more indicative of a lack of faith in God and his Word.

There is just one note of caution I want to strike. Not every promise in the Bible is for everyone throughout all generations. I cannot (nor would I want to) claim God's promise to Abraham and Sarah that they would have a child in their old age! Nor can I claim the plot of land currently known as Israel as my possession.

I have, in the past, claimed the promise that the Lord would restore the years the locust has eaten (Joel 2:25) though it originally applied to God's ancient people the Jews. My reason for doing this was simply that as I read it, it became alive to me in that way that scripture sometimes does so that you just *know* God is speaking to you. And God did keep that promise to me—years of what seemed like barrenness and fruitlessness in my spiritual life and ministry were followed by a deeper fellowship with God than I had previously known and unprecedented opportunities for ministry. God keeps his word. But I really am not sure about the man who claimed the promise of Isaiah 55 verse 12 when he wanted to ask a girl out who was blessed with the name of Joy!

So we can claim the general promises of God which he has made to all people and those which he has spoken to our own hearts, and doing so can be a great blessing to us because God delights to keep his promises.

There is one other point to keep in mind, and that is that some promises have a condition attached. God says if you will do this, then I will keep my promise. God's promise to never flood and destroy the entire earth again is unconditional; it is not dependent on our behaviour. An example of a conditional promise is found in James 5 verse 16:

> Therefore confess your sins to each other and pray for each other
> so that you may be healed.

I find it interesting how much healing ministry is conducted without encouraging the sick person to confess any sin. We seem to have almost completely lost the understanding that *some* sickness, but by no means *all* sickness, can be the result of sin. There are circumstances where no amount of faith-filled prayer will result in healing because there is an underlying sin problem. Again, let me stress that just because someone is prayed for and doesn't get well, it *does not necessarily mean* that the problem is unconfessed sin. However, James does make it clear that on at least some occasions confession of sin is a condition for God answering prayers for healing.

God keeps his promises, but we have to do our part.

Exercise

Look at Isaiah 9:6:

> For to us a child is born, to us a son is given, and the government
> will be on his shoulders. And he will be called Wonderful Counselor,
> Mighty God, Everlasting Father, Prince of Peace.

This prophetic passage describes the Lord Jesus. In particular, it gives four titles which tell us about his character. Think about how you might use these titles in prayer to ask him to meet your specific needs.

CHAPTER 19

Pleasing God

Here we find the secret of much unanswered prayer. We are not
listening to God's Word, and therefore He is not listening to our
petitions.

(RA Torrey)

Living a life of prayer means living a life of obedience to God and
pleasing him. The psalmist expresses this perfectly.

I have hidden your word in my heart that I might not sin against
you. (Ps. 119:11)

In Ephesians 5:10, Paul says this,

Find out what pleases the Lord.

If we are honest, most of us do not actively seek to find out what pleases
God. We do not pick up our Bibles with the intention of searching for things

we can do which will make the Lord happy. In fact, I would guess that we subconsciously hope that we won't come across something in our devotional time that might demand change from us.

Yet, here is an interesting thing. When it comes to the relationships we have with other human beings, we do actually try to find out what pleases the ones we love and then to act on that information—not because we are compelled to but because we want to. We carefully select the gifts we give them at birthday and Christmas; we treat them to their favourite meal. We dress to please them.

It really ought to be the same with the Lord. We should actually get pleasure from trying to find ways to please him. We should be searching the scriptures to discover the things that delight his heart and make him smile.

Have you ever read this passage?

> The LORD your God is with you, He is mighty to save. He will take great delight in you, He will quiet you with His love, He will rejoice over you with singing. (Zeph. 3:17)

Imagine the creator of the universe delighting in you and rejoicing over you with singing. If you knew he was doing that, wouldn't it transform your prayer life? Think of the joy you would experience in his presence if you knew he was pleased with you. If you please him through your obedience to his, word you will, as Torrey indicates above, find that he is more responsive to your prayers.

What I am *not* talking about here is strict adherence to Old Testament law simply because it is there. We are, after all, no longer under law but under grace (Rom. 6:14). The law had us duty bound to obedience while grace has us desiring to do right out of love for God for who he is and what he's done for us. As Paul says to the Corinthians in 2 Corinthians 5:9,

> We make it our goal to please Him.

LYNDA SCOTSON

So what does please the Lord, apart from the obvious things of staying clear of adultery and not murdering other people? When I decided to try to find out, I came up with a list of over thirty different things I could easily do which the Bible itself says cause pleasure to God. Let's look at one passage.

> For this reason, since the day we heard about you, we have not stopped praying for you and asking God to fill you with the knowledge of His will through all spiritual wisdom and understanding. And we pray this in order that you may live a life worthy of the Lord and may please Him in every way: bearing fruit in every good work, growing in the knowledge of God, being strengthened with all power according to His glorious might so that you may have great endurance and patience, and joyfully giving thanks to the Father, who has qualified you to share in the inheritance of the saints in the kingdom of light. (Col. 1:9-12)

See how Paul is praying for the Christians at Colossae and that part of that prayer is that they *may please Him in every way.* They are to do this in a number of ways, firstly by bearing fruit in their activities. It pleases God that we are active in service and that such service has positive outcomes. This doesn't have to be a major ministry. It pleases God when you cheer up a friend by calling to ask how they are or when you donate a little money to a Christian charity working with bereaved children.

The second thing that Paul lists as pleasing to God is growing in our knowledge of him. Sitting down to read our Bible or a Christian book, with the intention of understanding him better, pleases the Lord, as does spending time in his presence getting to know him more.

Thirdly, allowing the Lord to strengthen us so that we have endurance and patience is pleasing to him. When situations arise which exasperate us and we look to him for the resources to maintain our calm, we please him.

And finally it pleases him when we are thankful to him and joyful with it. Thankfulness is something most of us aren't very good at, let alone joy filled thankfulness. In this passage, Paul is talking about the thankfulness that comes from knowing we are saved. Over time, we can become quite blasé about our salvation and forget what we have been saved from, what we have gained, and just how much it has cost the Lord to redeem us. I think we probably need to reflect on this a little more than we do so that we are not simply thankful but joyful too.

Exercise

Set aside some time to search the Bible for ideas about how to please the Lord. One way to do this is to use an online Bible concordance such as biblegateway.com or blueletterbible.org and search for the words *please* and *God*. Some of the results will be relevant, others not. You can then try modifying your search terms slightly, replacing *please* with *pleasing* or *God* with *Lord* to find other references. If you don't have access to the Internet, you can use a regular concordance, but the job will take longer because you can only look up one word at a time.

CHAPTER 20

Praying Like Daniel

Now Daniel... went home to his upstairs room where the windows opened towards Jerusalem. Three times a day he got down on his knees and prayed, giving thanks to his God, just as he had done before.

(Dan. 6:10)

It has been drawn to my attention that Daniel is one of the few characters in the Bible about whom nothing negative is said. Indeed, it was the fact that no one could find any fault with Daniel that led to this very situation. There were people who wanted rid of Daniel, and they manipulated circumstances to their own ends.

The decree had come down from King Darius that only he should be worshipped during the next thirty days. This could have left Daniel with a serious dilemma. But Daniel was not a man of compromise when it came to his worship of God.

The key to Daniel's life was that it was centred on prayer. Prayer wasn't something he did because it was a duty nor was it something to be got out of the way at the beginning of the day so that he could then focus on the rest of his life. Prayer was integral to how he lived.

If Daniel, a refugee in an alien country, part of a persecuted minority, could maintain a consistent prayer life, we can surely learn something from his example. Let's look at this verse in some detail.

Firstly, Daniel set aside time for prayer not just once, or even twice, but three times a day. Even though he was a busy, high ranking government official, his life was saturated with prayer. He was going above and beyond what he might have felt obliged to do if he was trying to maintain the rhythm of temple worship. In the Temple, there were just two services a day, a morning and an evening sacrifice. But as we have already observed, men and women of God such as John Wesley, Desmond Tutu, and Madam Guyon have all attested to the importance of spending significant quantities of time in prayer when life and ministry become busy. Like them, Daniel recognised that the only way to do all that had to be done was to pray and to do so frequently. For Daniel, prayer was not something he simply fitted in when he could. It was scheduled, in his diary, and he kept the appointments he made with God.

The second thing to note is that Daniel had a *sacred space* where he went to pray. Deprived of Jerusalem and the Temple, he made his upper room a sanctuary where he met with God. As we discussed earlier, it is invaluable to have a particular place to pray because it is easier to settle, to take our focus off the world and place it firmly on God. To help him to remember who it was he was praying to, he chose a room which looked out towards the direction of Jerusalem. It wasn't a religious requirement for him to do so, as praying towards Mecca is for Muslims, but it probably helped him to feel connected to his homeland and his own people as he prayed to the God of his father's.

Then, thirdly, we read that Daniel knelt to pray. This powerful man with almost unrivalled authority in the land humbled himself physically, an outward act which reflected the inward attitude of his heart. This wasn't just because of the current desperate circumstances. Some people only get on their knees to pray when they are in particular need, when they are feeling desperate. But it was Daniel's daily practice to bow down in humility before his God. He recognised that God is always on the throne and that nations and empires rise and fall according to his will.

Fourthly, Daniel gave thanks to God. One might consider that in this dire situation, he would skip over that bit of prayer and move straight into the, *help me!* prayer. After all, he had been thanking God every day, and this was now a matter of urgency. Surely he needn't feel obliged to go through the motions of thanking God when he was in dreadful need. But no, Daniel stuck to his usual pattern. He gave thanks. I find that amazing. Only a man who truly knows his God is going to be trusting enough to keep the panic at bay and stick to his regular routine. His life is under threat, the lions are waiting, and Daniel gives thanks. He is acting out the instruction that Paul would later give to the followers of Christ in 1 Thessalonians 5:17-18:

> Pray continually; give thanks in all circumstances, for this is God's will for you in Christ Jesus.

So Daniel's example of determination to be thankful is not something just for the great men and women of God. It is something we are all to strive for.

Finally, and perhaps most importantly, we can see that Daniel had established a consistent prayer life over an extended period of time. He had learnt intimate communion with God. This wasn't a single act of defiance against those who wanted to see him brought down and executed. In fact, unless he already had an established prayer life, he could not have maintained the tranquillity of spirit to act as he did in the moment of crisis. Instead, it was a simple decision to keep doing what he'd always done. It appears not to have occurred to him to do anything else.

Elsewhere we see another great example of Daniel's prayer, but this is completely different and I just want to mention it in passing.

So I turned to the Lord God and pleaded with him in prayer and petition, in fasting, and in sackcloth and ashes. I prayed to the LORD my God and confessed. (Dan. 9:3-4)

Daniel had been studying Jeremiah's prophecy and realised that the time had come when God planned to restore his people to their own land. He also understood that it was because of the sins of the people that they had been taken into exile in the first place. We've already commented on Daniel's righteousness, so what he does next is quite remarkable. He identifies himself with the sin of the people. He prays and fasts and confesses as though he were one of the unrighteous multitudes who got Israel in the mess he was in. The following fifteen verses are a humble but passionate plea to God for forgiveness, recognising the Lord's righteousness and the people's sin. It puts our attempts at interceding for people to shame.

Exercise

It has been said that seven days without prayer makes one weak. How strong are you? Is there consistency in your prayer life? Have you come to the point in your walk with God that prayer comes naturally and it would be unthinkable to go a day without prayer? Ask God to help you become more consistent in your praying. Review what you are trying to do with your devotional times. Are they at the best time of day for you? Do you find the methods you are using fulfilling and satisfying? Would you benefit from making certain changes? Sometimes a minor modification can make a world of difference.

CHAPTER 21

Feeding on Jesus

How sweet the name of Jesus sounds
In a believer's ear.
It soothes his sorrows, heals his wounds,
And drives away his fear.

This hymn by John Newton, more famous for writing 'Amazing Grace' is one of my favourites because I have experienced the truth of its words.

Just recently, I had the privilege of being prayed for by a group of dear friends. It was wonderful to hear their love and concern through their prayers. But the thing which always touches me most at such times is hearing a brother or sister, eyes fixed on the Lord, whispering the name of Jesus under their breath. There is no name sweeter than that of our Saviour, and I've found that hearing it spoken tenderly from the lips of another believer does have a restorative effect on the soul.

It intrigues me that we sometimes seem so reticent to use this name. The Jews were, and still are, unwilling to use the name, Yahweh, that God gave to Moses by which he might be known. Their reluctance is perhaps understandable in the light of the third commandment which instructs against misusing the name of God. In a similar way, evangelical Christians often prefer to talk about 'God', 'Father', or 'The Lord' rather than to use the name of Jesus.

Yet the name of Jesus is absolutely central to our faith. It literally means *saviour*, and according to Peter (Acts 4:12), 'There is no other name under heaven given to men by which we must be saved.'

The Lord Jesus himself taught us that when we gather together in his name, he is there with us (Matt. 18:20). This is why, when we are struggling in any way, we should make an extra effort to meet and pray with our spiritual family. When we do, we are exposing ourselves to the healing presence of Jesus. The awareness of that awesome, gentle presence inevitably draws a response of worship most eloquently expressed by quietly speaking the most precious name of Jesus. It becomes the perfect prayer, especially when we are incapable of finding any other words. It becomes a way of feeding on Jesus, of being sustained by him.

> Then Jesus declared, 'I am the bread of life. He who comes to me will never go hungry.' (John 6:30)

After saying these words, Jesus goes on to talk about those who eat the bread of life having eternal life, but we should not make the assumption that he is simply talking about our need to *feed* on him for salvation. That is only part of the message.

The crowds that flocked to Jesus had been physically hungry, and he fed five thousand of them with just a few loaves and fish (John 6:1-15). They had experienced a miracle which had satisfied their bodies, but they were not satisfied spiritually. They thought they needed another miracle (verse 30). Instead Jesus taught them that he is the bread from heaven and that feeding on him is the source of eternal life (verse 57-58). Eternal life is not just our ultimate destiny, it is our present experience:

> This is eternal life: that they may know you, the only true God, and
> Jesus Christ whom you have sent. (John 17:3)

To feed on Jesus is to have eternal life which means to have experiential knowledge of him today.

We all have spiritual hunger though we sometimes try to satisfy it in the wrong way. We seek the company of friends, we look for sources of entertainment, we work for wealth, possessions, or status. There is nothing inherently wrong with any of these things, but if they are a substitute for feeding on Jesus, our spiritual hunger will never be satisfied.

I have found it is essential to my well-being and my ability to cope with the day that I spend a substantial amount of time fellowshipping with the Lord before I do anything else. Actually, I find it best if I don't even get out of bed until I've taken time to nourish my spirit with worship and Bible reading. If I fail to do that, I struggle with the day, and my family suffers because I become very short-tempered rather quickly.

I've come to the conclusion that the right amount of time for me to spend in feeding on Jesus is however long it takes for me to feel full. There comes a point when I know my spirit has received the nourishment it needs. To finish my prayer time before that leaves me spiritually weak for the rest of the day. To go beyond the point of feeling well fed is fruitless. I gain nothing extra from spending more time trying to pray. If I feel spiritually well fed after thirty minutes, there's no point carrying on for another half an hour just so I can tick a box that says I prayed an hour today.

We can learn a lot about feeding on Jesus by studying the way God provided manna to his people. Seven points emerge from the account in Exodus 16.

Firstly, it was a *heavenly supply*. Verse 4 tells us that the supply of manna was from heaven. In fact, Psalm 78:23-25 states that it was the bread of angels. Eating the manna sustained the Israelites physically. Feeding on Jesus, spending time in his presence and in his word, sustains us spiritually (John 6:27).

Secondly, it was a *daily supply*. Verse 4 also tells us that the manna was provided daily. The food gathered in the morning sustained the people throughout the day. Likewise we need to feed on Jesus daily, preferably as the first thing we do when we wake up, if we are to be sustained spiritually.

Thirdly, it was a *sufficient supply*. Verses 8, 12, 18 show us that the manna was sufficient, whatever the need. The day before Jesus claimed, 'I am the bread of life,' he had fed 5,000 people with five loaves and two fish. We can keep gathering our bread until we are replete. In our feeding on Jesus, we should aim to gather from him until we have eaten sufficient to satisfy our spirit. Equally, if we find enough quickly, the wise thing to do is digest it rather than to keep gathering more.

Fourthly, it was an overflowing supply. Verse 16 indicates that the people gathered not just for themselves but also for dependents. When we feed on Jesus, we will be able to gather enough to overflow into other people's lives. Hebrews 5:11-14 tells us we should grow up to become teachers ourselves. The question is, are you one of those who looks to feed from the supply others have gathered, or are you one of those who attracts people seeking what you have gathered?

Fifthly it was a fresh supply. Verse 5 shows how manna needed to be gathered daily. Except for the Sabbath, they could not be sustained by what had been collected the previous day. Nor can we live indefinitely on what the Lord has given us in the past. We need something fresh from the Lord each day. We need the whole counsel of God's Word, not just our favourite passages of scripture. 2 Timothy 3:16 says,

> All Scripture is God-breathed and is useful for teaching, rebuking, correcting and training in righteousness.

In Deuteronomy 8:3, Moses explains to Israel that one purpose of the daily supply of manna was *To teach you that man does not live on bread alone but on every word that comes from the mouth of God.*

There is so much in scripture that there will always be a fresh supply to sustain us spiritually.

Sixthly, it was a *mysterious supply*. Verses 15, 31 reveal that the Israelites did not know what the manna was. In fact, the very word, *manna* means, *what is it?* The Lord Jesus, when speaking to the church in Pergamum, refers to hidden manna (Rev. 2:17). The sustenance we receive from feeding on Jesus and his Word is not something that can be adequately explained or described. But those who live on the bread of heaven know how powerful and effective it is.

Finally, it is a sweet supply. Verse 31 also tells us that the manna tasted like *wafers made with honey*. Psalm 119:103 says, *How sweet are your words to my taste.* Psalm 34:8 says, *Taste and see that the Lord is good.* Psalm 19:10 describes God's laws as *sweeter than honey*. Our times of feeding on Jesus are meant to be very sweet.

The *feeding on Jesus* that I've described here is simply a personal devotional time. I found very early in my Christian experience that trying to include praying for others in the same slot as praying for myself didn't work. I would be enjoying the Lord's company and then start to feel guilty because I wasn't mentioning the needs of others. Or I would be praying for friends, family, and Christian workers but feel frustrated because I was neglecting feeding on Jesus.

What I have found most beneficial is to have two separate prayer times, one for just me and the Lord at the beginning of the day and a second period later in the day which I devote solely to praying for others. That way, I feel I am giving my best to both my personal relationship with the Lord and to my intercession for others.

Exercise

Are your times with Jesus sweet? Do they sustain you throughout the day? Do you find you discover things that help others as well as yourself? If you do, you will need no encouragement to persist in feeding on him. If not, do not be discouraged. Ask the Lord to satisfy your hunger for him each time you turn to him in prayer. Press on, daily feeding on him and his Word. You will grow to appreciate those precious times of sweetness.

CHAPTER 22

A Write Way to Pray

One thing I ask of the Lord,

This is what I seek:

That I may dwell in the house of the Lord

All the days of my life,

To gaze upon the beauty of the Lord

And to seek him in his temple.

Hear my voice when I call, O Lord;

Be merciful to me and answer me.

My heart says of you, 'Seek his face!'

Your face, Lord, I will seek.

(Ps. 27:4, 7-8)

Human beings are creatures of habit, so we tend to repeatedly do the same things in the same way. Often it doesn't matter. It's not really important, for example, if we always sit in the same place at church. But we shouldn't allow our prayer lives to get into that kind of rut. We should be growing and moving forward, developing our intimacy with the Lord and closeness with our brothers and sisters. The church prayer time which always follows the same pattern and always prays around the same topics will become stifled. I have seen it happen. Over time people begin to lose their passion for prayer and either come only out of duty or stop attending altogether.

One thing that can be said of David's prayers is that they are never boring. We can learn a lot about how to reinvigorate our prayer times by studying his approach. For example, he is quite willing to tell God exactly how he's feeling and what he thinks of the way other people are treating him. He hides nothing from God.

Not only is David very liberated in his prayers, frequently moving between talking to God, speaking to others, or addressing his own soul, he has clearly often thought carefully about what to pray and worked at creating a poetic structure. Psalm 9, for example, is an acrostic poem with each stanza beginning with successive letters of the Hebrew alphabet. As someone who's dabbled in writing poetry, I can tell you that that kind of construction takes hard work as well as inspiration.

We benefit from the fact that David committed his psalms to writing. I'm sure this fact blessed David himself as he was able to look back over past prayers and see how the Lord had responded.

In the past, I have kept journals which have been a record of my walk with the Lord. It is very encouraging to review them and see answers to prayer and how I have grown in my spiritual life. It is also quite common for me to slip into prayer as I write so, like David, I have records of prayers I prayed in the past.

More recently, I have taken to writing letters to the Lord Jesus. It is a completely different spiritual experience to praying aloud or praying silently in one's own heart, and I find it to be hugely beneficial for a number of reasons.

The first is that writing takes more care than spoken prayer. It takes longer to write than to speak, and you have to be clear in your own mind what you want to say. So you slow down and think about what you're praying. You can be carefully revising and rewriting your thoughts so that they express exactly what you mean.

Slowing down and taking time means that you relax into the prayer time. I find it easier to worship because I can meditate on the Lord and think about those aspects of him that are worthy of praise. As I write, one expression of worship flows into the next. For example, while I am writing about worshipping God as Creator, all sorts of aspects of that creation come to mind. I may begin by thinking about the wonders of the natural world and move from there to mountains and waters, then to the creatures of the sea, to the varieties of fish, the beauty of the coral reefs, and so on. Because I have had to slow down my expression of worship, my mind has more time to expand the thoughts I have about the magnificence of our creator-God.

Slowing down also means that my heart is more open to hear the Lord's voice. Many times I've written about something that concerns me, and as I have expressed myself on paper, the answer has been whispered to my spirit. I have numerous letters where I have poured out my heart about something and have ended up thanking the Lord for his Word which has come to me as I've written. Such times are very precious.

I have also discovered, like David, that writing to the Lord is a very effective way of dealing with hurt and anger. Putting down on paper the stark reality of what I am feeling pulls me up short. I have the freedom to be totally honest, and I can sometimes be shocked by what has poured from my heart. This leads me more easily into forgiveness and repentance than the constant mulling over of these things before God in my mind. Somehow, putting them down on paper, releasing them from being trapped inside of me, enables me to hand them over to Jesus and leave them there. Instead of guilt-laden thoughts that keep returning, I have a record of my confession and repentance, a reminder that the deed has been done and I am free.

If you like to use the computer or your smartphone for emailing, you might like to consider the idea of setting up an email address to send your letters to. Now I know this might sound on a par with children's letters to Santa. Of course, you don't need to send your letters anywhere. The Lord Jesus sees them whatever you do. But I find I get a sense of completion by hitting the 'send' button, otherwise I would be returning constantly to what I'd written to amend it, even weeks afterwards. For me, sending the email is like the 'amen' at the end of a spoken prayer. It says, 'Yes, that really is what I want to say and now I'm done.'

Exercise

Read the devotion, A Love Letter to Jesus. Then take pen and paper, and write your own letter to God. Be yourself, say what you think, direct your words to whichever person of the Trinity you feel most comfortable with.

CHAPTER 23

Journaling

It seemed good to me to write an orderly account.

(Luke 1:2)

I have already suggested the idea of journaling, but I now want to expand on that because a journal or diary can be used to aid prayer in a number of ways.

How often do you promise to pray for someone and then forget? You really did mean to pray for that person, but the busyness of life squeezed it out of your memory. The next time you see them, they thank you for your prayers, saying that they've been answered, and you are left wondering whether you should confess your forgetfulness. Carrying a small notebook and pencil with you means that you can write down prayer requests immediately, and mental lapses are far less likely to occur. You can use such a notebook in prayer meetings and services too.

You can also use a journal or diary to divide up the week or month so that you pray specifically for certain people, circumstances, or ministries on particular days. That way, you don't feel the heavy load of trying to pray for everyone every day. Spreading out the prayer load like this means that you can spend more concentrated time on each, being specific in your prayers.

It is also beneficial to write down anything you think the Lord might be saying to you as you pray or listen to teaching, whether through scripture or direct to your heart. Do it straight away, and you will have a permanent and accurate record of what God has said that can be referred to later on. Write everything down which you feel he might be speaking into your spirit—sometimes God says something which doesn't make sense to us at the time but which we may come to understand much later.

A journal is also good for recording dreams. I'm not a believer that every dream has something to say to us from the Lord. The vast majority of dreams are simply our brain processing and filing away the events of the day. On occasions, I've dosed off listening to the radio or watching TV only to wake up and realise my dreams had contained and been directed by the news. However, God spoke to people in dreams in scripture, and I believe that he has sometimes spoken to me through dreams. In my experience, you don't need someone to interpret your dreams for you; nor do you need a handbook telling you what different elements of a dream might mean. On the few occasions God has spoken to me through a dream, I have woken as soon as the dream ended and immediately knew what it meant without having to even think about it, let alone analyse it. Let me offer you an example of this. It was the first time, that I am aware of, that I had a dream with a spiritual meaning.

Many years ago, I dreamt I was looking into a room, which was so swamped with books that at first I did not see the table with the cross on it. It was only as I took care to look properly that I saw the cross. I woke up straight away and knew that God was saying to me that I should not get so distracted by theology and the study of religion that I lose sight of what is essential—the cross. That had a profound effect on me.

So if you wake in the night having had a dream which seems to have been planted in your mind by the Holy Spirit, write it down immediately. You will be able to take it into your next devotional time and respond to it thoughtfully and prayerfully.

Another extremely valuable use for a journal is to use it to write about what has gone on in your day and your reactions to those events. As with writing letters to God, it slows your thinking down and enables you to reflect on how you might have handled things better. You can note specific prayers you have prayed and record when they have been answered.

However you use a journal, you should respect yourself and your relationship with God enough to keep it private. Don't leave it lying around, offering a temptation to someone else to pick it up. Your communications with God are as private as those with a spouse.

Exercise

Buy yourself a notebook. Get yourself a piece of paper and make a list of all the things and people you want to pray about regularly. Next to each one, write down the frequency with which you want to pray for them—daily, weekly, monthly. Head the first page of the notebook, *Daily*, and list on that page everything you plan to pray for on a daily basis. Head the next seven pages with the days of the week, *Sunday, Monday, Tuesday*, and so on. Then allocate each of your weekly prayer items to a particular day. Finally, write the numbers 1 to 31 on the following pages, and write each of your monthly items on one of these pages. On the first day of a new month, you will be praying for those things and people on the page headed with a 1, on the second day those on the page headed 2, and so on. When there are only thirty days in a month, you may choose to bring forward the items for day thirty-one to day thirty. This method will make February twenty-eighth a busy day for prayer, so I would suggest you list fewer items for days twenty-eight, twenty-nine, thirty, and thirty-one than for the rest of the month.

So this is how it will work. If the fifth day of the month falls on a Tuesday, you will be praying for all the items on your daily list, plus those on the page headed Tuesday and the one headed with a number five.

Don't be afraid to add things, cross things out, or move them around. It is your tool to aid you in praying for others. Don't let it dictate to you. Always be flexible.

CHAPTER 24

Shout!

Shout for joy to the Lord, all the earth.

(Ps. 98:4, Ps. 100:1)

I can't honestly say there are that many times when I've shouted for joy to the Lord, but there have been occasions when I've found that raising my voice has been extremely beneficial.

The Hebrew word translated as *shout* in these verses is *rua*, which literally means *to raise a battle cry*. That might seem a surprising thing for the psalmist to say: Raise a battle cry for joy to the Lord. But perhaps when we consider the reasons for battle cries, it will make more sense.

Battle cries have two main functions. The first is to instill courage and passion in those going into the fight. You know the kind of thing. In the words of William Shakespeare,

Cry, 'God for Harry, England and Saint George!' [*Henry V* (Act III, Scene I)]

The closest Biblical equivalent is found in 2 Chronicles 13:12.

> God is with us; He is our leader. His priests with their trumpets will
> sound the battle cry against you.

The common factor in these two cries is that God is with us, he is on our side, the implication being that we are therefore undefeatable, and so should have courage.

The second function of a battle cry is to put fear into the heart of the enemy. Who would not quake and tremble before an army charging down the hill (you've seen the movies), shouting at the tops of their voices and brandishing their weapons?

> And the men of Judah raised the battle cry. At the sound of their
> battle cry, God routed Jeroboam and all Israel before Abijah and
> Judah. (2 Chron. 13:15)

When we're facing the storms of life, the temptation can be to emulate the disciples and cower in the bottom of the boat while we wait for the trouble to go away or for Jesus to rescue us. Whilst it is true that we must turn to the Lord in difficult times, that doesn't mean that we run away from the challenges. We must remind ourselves who is on our side—Jesus who is the Lion of the Tribe of Judah and who has already triumphed (Rev. 5:5). We must also remind ourselves who we are and that we are *more than conquerors* through him who loved us (Rom. 8:37).

Our enemy, the devil, is only *like* a roaring lion (1 Pet. 5:8). He has to work hard to try to make us feel overwhelmed, inadequate, and vulnerable so that we are of no use to the Lord. Our response must be to raise a battle cry that will strengthen our spirits and enable us to stand and take the fight to him.

Psalm 47:5 says that God has ascended amidst shouts of joy. When we make our battle cry, we exalt the Lord and bring glory to him. In difficult times, we may not feel like being joyful, but scripture tells us to rejoice in the Lord always (Phil. 4:4) because when we do our focus is on El Shaddai, the Almighty God who is big enough to lead us into victory in all the circumstances of our lives.

This is all very well, but what does it mean to raise a battle cry in practice? There are all sorts of ways to do this that will help us to stand up under the struggles we face and to win the victory. One is simply to *shout for joy to the Lord*. Yes, actually raise your voice and shout out praises to God. If that is just a bit too *off the wall* for you, you might try playing some praise CDs loud enough that you can join in and let rip with everything you've got. Fill your lungs with air and let rip. I've found that the car is an excellent place to do this as it doesn't disturb too many people, though the family hasn't always agreed with me! Whatever you do, give it your all. Just the fact of filling your lungs with enough air to belt out a good praise song will make you feel better, and confessing the truth about our awesome God will build you up spiritually.

Actually, most of us are so timid that simply speaking scripture aloud is a challenge for us. We tend to think that having a quiet time means being silent and still. That very phrase may inhibit us from having the liberty to break the sound barrier and open our mouths. There is a great deal of benefit to be had from reading aloud passages of scripture, which talk about our victory over our enemy. The end of Romans chapter 8 makes an excellent battle cry, and it almost demands to be spoken aloud, if not shouted.

Who shall separate us from the love of Christ? Shall trouble or hardship or persecution or famine or nakedness or danger or sword? As it is written: For your sake we face death all day long; we are considered as sheep to be slaughtered. No, in all these things we are more than conquerors through him who loved us. For I am convinced that neither death nor life, neither angels nor demons, neither the present nor the future, nor any powers, neither height nor depth, nor anything else in all creation, will be able to separate us from the love of God that is in Christ Jesus our Lord. (Rom. 8:35-39)

Exercise

Take your Bible and go to the car, the bathroom, a nearby park, or anywhere else you feel comfortable that you will not attract undue attention by speaking aloud. Turn to Psalm 100 and read verses 1 and 2 quietly to yourself. Then read them aloud, but in a whisper. Read them again at the level of normal conversational speech. Keep reading them, increasing the volume a little each time until you have reached a level where you are conscious that you have a sense of liberation.

CHAPTER 25

Pray About Everything

You don't have what you want because you don't ask God for it.

(James 4:2)

You may ask me for anything in my name, and I will do it.

(John 14:14)

But seek first His kingdom and His righteousness, and all these things [that you need] will be given to you as well.

(Matt. 6:33)

Ask and it will be given to you; seek and you will find; knock and the door will be opened to you.

(Matt. 7:7)

My youngest son was nine, and he had really grasped the principle behind the teaching of Jesus in Luke 11:5-8:

> Then He said to them, Suppose one of you has a friend, and he goes
> to him at midnight and says, 'Friend, lend me three loaves of bread,
> because a friend of mine on a journey has come to me, and I have
> nothing to set before him.' Then the one inside answers, 'Don't bother
> me. The door is already locked, and my children are with me in bed.
> I can't get up and give you anything.' I tell you, though he will not get
> up and give him the bread because he is his friend, yet because of the
> man's boldness he will get up and give him as much as he needs.

His persistence in asking for a particular item over several weeks was a perfect illustration of this text. He knows that he can ask for anything. He won't always get what he asks for; he doesn't always understand what's best for himself. But as his parent, it is my responsibility to make the decisions about when to give and when to withhold. And if I withhold, I always explain why.

In childlike faith, we can come to our heavenly Father and ask for anything, knowing that he will say *yes* if it's right for us and *no* if it's not. And if we pay attention, we will usually hear his explanation. Sometimes the answer will not be *yes* or *no*, but *this is what you need to do in order to receive what you want*.

It's not our problem to try to work out what God wants to give us before we decide whether or not to ask for it. Simply ask, in the childlike way that my son does, and wait for the answer. God is not an ogre who's going to tell us off if we ask for the wrong thing. But he does want us to come and ask, both for what we want and what we need. As James says, sometimes the only reason we don't have these things is because we haven't asked.

Let me tell you about a jaw-droppingly amazing answer to prayer, which our family experienced a few years ago. It's not my intention to boast but to illustrate how God loves to give good gifts to his children (Matt. 7:11).

For some time, our growing (in size, not number!) family had been complaining every time we tried to squeeze all five of us into our Ford Escort. I loved that car. It was nippy. You put your foot down, and it went, unlike its predecessor which almost seemed to be saying, *do we have to?* whenever it pulled away. There was absolutely nothing wrong with the Escort except that it had become too small. The general consensus in the family was that we needed something bigger. But there was simply no way we could afford to replace the car.

So I started praying for a new car. I could have just asked for a bigger car, but having recently been challenged about being specific in prayer and asking the Lord for what you really want, I decided to ask for a red (yes, red) people carrier. Why red? Simply because every car I'd ever owned had been one shade or another of blue, and all of us wanted a change. Childish? Maybe, but aren't we supposed to come to God as our heavenly Father? And he's quite capable of saying *no* if we're asking for the wrong thing.

I didn't mention the request for the new car every day in my prayer time. I didn't plead for it with any great fervour. I simply asked, every so often, over a period of six months, *please can we have a red people carrier*, and occasionally I would remind the Lord how much we needed it—most frequently when all three children (two of whom were adult size by this time) were squeezed in the back of the Escort.

Then, completely out of the blue, a family member, who knew nothing of my prayers and isn't even a Christian, phoned and asked me to look at a silver Nissan that was for sale at their local dealership. I explained that, yes we did need a bigger car, but there was no way we could afford to buy one at the moment. He said he'd like us to take a look at it anyway. But by the time we got there, the vehicle had been sold.

Well, it hadn't actually been a people carrier, and it certainly wasn't red, so I wasn't greatly disappointed. But our benefactor declared that if he could find the right car at the right price, he would buy it for us. So I sat back and waited while he made calls, looked in the newspaper, and surfed the net hunting down second-hand seven-seater vehicles. Every single one he found was too old or the mileage was too high or the price was unreasonable or it had a dubious history. He looked at dozens of adverts for cars, but the first one he found that he thought was worth looking at was a five-year-old *red* people carrier!

I was excited. But we were on holiday in Taunton, and the car was 140 miles away, in Walsall, just twenty minutes drive from our home! My husband phoned the seller to find out if it was still available. It was, but the owner himself was going on holiday the next day. We made a decision. This was too good an opportunity to miss. We jumped in the car and were inspecting the potential purchase within three hours of first making contact with the seller.

To cut a very long story slightly shorter, we drove back to Taunton the following day in a red people carrier, which had cost us not a single penny.

I learnt so many things about prayer through that experience. Here are just some of them.

Yes, do be specific in prayer. Not only does our heavenly Father love to give good gifts to his children, the little details help give you confidence that you've found the right answer.

Prayer is not complicated. You don't have to find the right form of words, take up a particular posture, or even have oodles of faith. Simply ask for what you want and wait and see what God will do.

Persistence in prayer doesn't require you to nag God. We should keep asking, but we don't have to take the, *can I have a new car please, can I have a new car please, can I have a new car please* approach that children sometimes do.

Seek first the Kingdom of God. When you are praying diligently for God's Kingdom to be extended, you get more answers to personal requests.

Seek his righteousness. Obey God in even the small things. A few weeks before the answer came, I felt God was challenging me to drive within the speed limit, something I struggle with as I like to get everywhere as quickly as possible. But I made a real effort to get my driving speed down, and whilst I sometimes forget and the speed creeps up, I'm getting better at it. I didn't make the connection at the time between my prayer request and that decision to be obedient, and it certainly wasn't a case of trying to twist God's arm by being extra good! But I now wonder if we would have been given the car if I hadn't responded to the prompting of the Spirit to be more righteous in my driving.

Don't go running on ahead, be patient. We actually looked at the possibility of hiring a people carrier for the holiday and borrowing the money to pay for it! Instead we had our very own people carrier for most of the holiday, and beyond, and it was free.

God's not going to allow anyone else to get their hands on your blessing. If it's meant for you, he will keep it for you. This car had been up for sale for at least five weeks—listed on a well-known car trade site on the web and with three *For Sale* posters in the car. The seller had not had a single enquiry about it until we contacted him.

The Lord can use anyone, even unbelievers, to bless his people. The seller was not a Christian, the benefactor is not a Christian, but the Lord brought the two of them together to pour out a blessing on his children.

God's resources are not limited by our circumstances. The day before the original phone call from our generous relative, a verse in Jeremiah had leapt off the page during my quiet time—*they will find blessings even in the barren land* (Jer. 31:2). I didn't know what the Lord was specifically saying, but I knew it was something to do with blessing us where we couldn't provide for ourselves. That's exactly what happened.

The kind of dramatic answer to prayer I've described here doesn't happen to us every day or even every year. But it does illustrate how, when we partner with God in prayer, miracles can happen in the lives of ordinary believers. Whatever it is you're asking the Lord for, take encouragement from this personal story and persist in prayer.

However, there are times when God says *no*. There are all sorts of reasons why our prayers are not answered in the way we would like them to be. But we can learn and grow through unanswered prayer.

I've often heard it said that it is not helpful to ask God the *why* question and that we should simply trust him to work in our lives in his way and in his time.

Many times, that is true. We all go through phases of our lives when apparently inexplicable things happen to us, and it seems that the Lord has failed to respond to our cry of desperation in our darkest hour. Our faith in a loving heavenly Father is stretched, and we can either grow or crumble.

However if we are not getting answers to our prayers, we need to know if there is some fault on our part, a failure in us that we can rectify in order to get us to a place where our prayers will be answered. I learnt this lesson many years ago whilst praying for friends who desperately wanted a child but were failing to conceive.

As I prayed with Kathy (names have been changed to protect the identity of those concerned), I felt prompted to ask the Lord to show us if there was anything hindering the answer to our prayers. The Lord gently spoke to her heart through the story of the birth of Samuel. He revealed to her that she was seeking to fulfill her own maternal desires while God wanted to give her a child she could dedicate to him. Kathy responded to the Lord, and within a year, her own son was born, and she appropriately named him Samuel. It wasn't long before she had a daughter too.

The key to Kathy's prayer for a child was in her willingness to hear the Lord explain why there had not yet been an answer.

There are innumerable reasons why we might be the hindrance to our own prayers or even to the prayers other people are praying for us. We need to be open to whatever the Holy Spirit wants to communicate to our hearts about our personal walk with him. But there are some basic problems which, it seems to me, keep recurring.

The first and perhaps most obvious is unconfessed sin. Jesus responded to the paralysed man's need for healing by saying, *your sins are forgiven* (Matt. 9:1-8), and James also relates forgiveness and healing when he talks about the elders anointing the sick (Jas. 5:13-16).

That is not to say that sin is always the reason for unanswered prayers in relation to sickness. In my personal experience, it is sometimes a case of enforced rest. The Lord allows us to be *set aside* for a while because we need physical or spiritual refreshment, and we're too willful to take the time out without him imposing it upon us. I've seen this happen in the lives of others too. It's as though the Lord has said, *Sit down and shut up for a minute and let me talk to you.* Isn't this more or less what happened to Saul on the road to Damascus (Acts 9:1-19)?

The final thing I want to mention is that sometimes the Lord doesn't answer our prayers because we haven't yet learnt all we need to learn in the situation in which we find ourselves. Perhaps we're not seeing a breakthrough in our finances because we haven't yet learnt the lessons God wants to teach us about living a simple life, sacrificial giving, or trusting him to supply all our needs. Perhaps there are problems in our marriage because we haven't learnt to live out the roles defined in scripture, our love for our partner is greater than that we have for the Lord, or we haven't truly learnt to forgive.

The reasons for unanswered prayer will be uniquely personal to our individual circumstances and our walk with the Lord. But if we are prepared to ask the Lord why he hasn't responded in the way we have asked, and are willing to be humble enough to hear his voice and respond, unanswered prayer can be the key to significant spiritual growth.

Exercise

Spend some time reflecting on whether there are things you haven't asked your heavenly Father for because you weren't sure if you should. Then take some time to simply ask God for those things. Be prepared for him to give you his answer and his explanation, and if he requires you to act, then do so.

If you are experiencing the frustration of unanswered prayer, try praying, *Lord, is there something in me that needs to change before you will say yes?* Make sure you listen for the answer and respond when it comes.

CHAPTER 26

What to Do When You Don't Know What to Do

I know the plans I have for you, declares the Lord, plans to prosper
you and not to harm you, plans to give you hope and a future.

(Jer. 29:11)

This is a very well-known verse in the midst of a passage that is not so
well known. It's comforting and encouraging when we don't understand what's
going on in our lives. It has often been directed my way in difficult times. But
when these words were originally spoken through the prophet, he actually told
them precisely what was going on.

Jeremiah had told the exiles from Jerusalem, taken away by Nebuchadnezzar,
that they were to spend seventy years in Babylon. This was not what the people
wanted to hear. They wanted to believe the words of the false prophets telling
them everything would be all right.

I expect most people were just plain confused. They would have had a hard
time deciding who to listen to and how they should respond. They were simply

ordinary people apparently caught up in the plans of the political powers of the day—just pawns on the chessboard. Their lives had been turned upside down, they had lost loved ones, been dragged away from their ancestral homes to an unfamiliar land with unfamiliar laws and practices. They didn't feel like people with a hope and a destiny (which is what the Hebrew word translated *future* actually means).

Jeremiah brought these poor disillusioned people two great words from the Lord. The first was, *get on with life*. He tells them to settle down and live their lives. Build homes, he says, plant gardens, have children, give them in marriage, and seek the prosperity of the city where you live. In other words, don't behave any differently to the way you would in your homeland. That's a sobering word for anyone waiting expectantly for the Lord to change their circumstances in some way. Don't put your life on hold while you wait for God's intervention. Carry on with the daily routine—work, bring up your family, and trust that he will bring about any necessary change in his own good time.

That's the first part of the programme. The second part is what this book is all about. In verses 12 to 13, we have a call to prayer with the promise that *you will seek me and find me when you seek me with all your heart*. Whilst the people go on living as normal, they are not to neglect God. Rather, they are to give themselves over to seeking God with everything they've got.

There are a number of important points to be drawn from this. The first is that they are not told to pray for deliverance or change but simply to seek God. He wants their hearts set on him and not on their own hopes and desires. How easy it is for us to focus on circumstances we're not comfortable with and to concentrate our prayers on that instead of worshipping the Lord and seeking his face?

The second point is that they are to seek him with *all their hearts*. It is an undivided focus on God, and it is not an intellectual seeking to understand his will or his ways. They are to seek an encounter with the Lord and to keep seeking until they find him.

Thirdly, they cannot find him simply by striving. In verse 14, the Lord says, *I will be found by you.* The mental image I have is of a father playing hide-and-seek with a young child. The child cannot find the father if he hides himself well but, in the spirit of the game and because he loves his child, he will make himself easy to find. Our heavenly Father wants to be found by us and so allows himself to be found when we've done our part by searching him out.

My youngest son is constantly searching me out to give me a hug. I will be lying down for a rest, working in the office on the computer, or preparing a meal in the kitchen, and he will track me down simply for the pleasure of a hug and to say that he loves me. This is the picture we are given in these verses. This is the kind of prayer the Lord wants from us, seeking him out to say we love him, not to complain about our circumstances, or to ask for change.

Having told the people to live out their ordinary lives, as they would have done at home, and to seek him wholeheartedly in prayer, the Lord says, *I will bring you back . . . I will gather you.*

There is a very profound teaching here. If we don't like our circumstances it is not *our* responsibility to try to change things. Our role is to carry on with normal daily life, seek the face of God in prayer, and trust him to bring his will to pass. That is not as passive as it may sound. There is nothing passive about getting on with life or spending serious amounts of time in prayer. Passivity is saying, I'm doing nothing until I get some clear guidance. This is not God's way.

Isaiah, the other great Old Testament prophet, brought this word from God,

> Whether you turn to the right or to the left, your ears will hear a voice
> behind you saying, this is the way, walk in it. (Is. 30:21)

It is as we walk through ordinary life that the Lord directs us. You can't steer a stationary car; nor can you get guidance while you're sitting around, waiting for something to happen. Neither will you hear that still, small voice of direction as you walk, unless you have learnt to recognise it in the time spent seeking God with all your heart in your prayer times.

Exercise

So this is what you do when you don't know what to do. Number one, keep on living your normal, ordinary daily life; number two, seek God with all your heart, not for answers, but simply to know him, to love him, and to learn the sound of his voice. Whatever challenges you are facing at the moment, decide now that you are not going to give up on either of these things.

CHAPTER 27

Have You Hur'd?

I want men everywhere to lift up holy hands in prayer.

(1 Tim. 2:8)

The theme of raising hands in prayer or worship is repeated throughout the Old and New Testaments. I did hear one young man use this particular verse to argue that women were not to raise their hands at all, but that just shows you can make scripture say anything you want it to if you take verses out of context.

Probably the most familiar passage about hands being raised in prayer is Exodus 17:8-13:

> The Amalekites came and attacked the Israelites at Rephidim. Moses said to Joshua, Choose some of our men and go out to fight the Amalekites. Tomorrow I will stand on top of the hill with the staff of God in my hands. So Joshua fought the Amalekites as Moses had ordered, and Moses, Aaron and Hur went to the top of the hill. As long as Moses held up his hands, the Israelites were winning, but whenever he lowered his hands, the Amalekites were winning. When

Moses's hands grew tired, they took a stone and put it under him and he sat on it. Aaron and Hur held his hands up—one on one side, one on the other—so that his hands remained steady till sunset. So Joshua overcame the Amalekite army with the sword.

This is the account of Joshua's defeat of the Amalekites as Moses stood on a hill overlooking the battlefield. When he held up his hands, the Israelites were winning; when he grew tired and lowered his arms, the battle turned against them.

If you've ever tried standing for any length of time with your arms in the air, you will realise how quickly they begin to tire and ache. There was a simple and practical solution to this problem. Two men, Aaron and Hur, took the responsibility of holding up Moses's weary arms until the battle was won.

The account is often used by preachers as an illustration of the importance of both prayer and action in working to achieve God's will. It's a valid use of the passage, but there is an additional insight here which could transform the effectiveness of the prayer of the church.

We are all supposed to pray for ourselves, for friends and family, for the extension of God's Kingdom. But you can't be in fellowship with other believers for long without realising that some Christians seem to have a particular passion for praying for others. They're easy to spot because, as I've said before, they are the ones who take out notebooks the minute someone starts to mention needs for prayer.

These gifted intercessors can spend hours in prayer asking the Lord to intervene in all kinds of situations from the personal to the international. Most of what they do is in the secret place so the rest of the fellowship will probably be unaware of the amount of time and commitment such people give to prayer; nor will they appreciate the physical and spiritual toll such a ministry can take on the individual intercessor.

It's also true that intercession is one of the most underrated ministries within the church. The work of the intercessor may well be the crucial difference between success or failure of a venture the church is undertaking; the effectiveness of the preacher or worship leader may be significantly enhanced as a result of intercession. The number and severity of spiritual attacks on church members can be reduced by the actions of the gifted prayers.

There is a lot of talk these days about preventative medicine—preventing medical problems by intervening before they arise. An example might be encouraging people to give up smoking so as to avoid lung cancer. I believe there is a role for preventative prayer—praying for protection from the various onslaughts of the enemy before they occur. This is one of the vital roles of intercessors.

Several times recently, I have heard gifted intercessors talk about becoming weary and finding it more difficult to pray than they used to. Like Moses, they have found it impossible to maintain their part of the battle because they haven't had the support they need. This is my observation, not theirs. I believe it is because intercessors are at the sharp end of the battle, on the spiritual front line, and they need support, care, and encouragement.

Pastors particularly have a responsibility to support the intercessors of the church. Just like Aaron the priest, Moses's brother, they have a role to play in enabling the prayers to keep praying. It's all too easy to think that the people who pray effectively are in less need of pastoral care than those whose spiritual or personal life appears more unstable. But intercessors, by the very nature of their ministry, are vulnerable too, and the spiritual leaders of the community must support them as Aaron supported Moses.

The other man assisting Moses was Hur. We know very little about him though Jewish tradition suggests he was Miriam's husband. He did not have the same kind of prominent role in the community as Moses or Aaron. But he was on that hill with them supporting Moses through his prayer vigil.

The intercessors in our churches need people like Hur. They need friends and companions who will quietly encourage them whilst both praying with and for them, ordinary people without leadership roles in the church. I have noticed there tends to be a general respect for the intercessors and sometimes an awe of their ability to pray as though they are somehow superior Christians. But of course, they are simply members of the family who just happen to have been given a particular role to fulfill. Our respect for them needs to be translated into prayer.

Leaving the intercessors to themselves and letting them just get on with their ministry will lead to a weak and ineffective church. When the intercessors are being encouraged and prayed for by their pastors and other church members, they will become more effective and the entire ministry of the church will flourish and become more dynamic.

Exercise

Who will pray for the prayers? Our intercessors need prayer. Will you be a Hur? If you don't already know who the gifted intercessors in your church are, find out who they are. Then start praying for them that the Lord will strengthen and encourage them, that he will protect them and that their ministry will be effective.

CHAPTER 28

Building a Foundation for Answered Prayer

If my people, who are called by my name, will humble themselves and pray and seek my face and turn from their wicked ways, then I will hear from heaven and will forgive their sin and will heal their land.

(2 Chron. 7:14)

Prayer is indeed like a many-faceted jewel. There are so many different ways to pray so much that can be learnt only through praying. Yet I have this feeling that we have mostly looked at it from one perspective and haven't yet discovered the myriad of delights which can be perceived from other angles.

The focus of this book has primarily been on personal prayer and building our own relationship with the Lord Jesus Christ. The reason is because I believe that without a firm foundation in our life with him, we cannot truly pray with any degree of faith or any confidence that we are praying according to his will. The same Lord who said, *remain in me and I in you*, also said, in the same discourse, *apart from me you can do nothing*, (John 15:1-5). That includes effective prayer.

The first purpose of prayer is to develop our relationship with God, to set down our roots in a life with him. In prayer, we see the awful contrast between his perfect holiness and our sin. In prayer, we recognise our weakness and his almighty strength. In prayer, we discover the lavishness of his love compared with the poverty of our own. In short, in prayer we gain a correct perspective of our creatureliness before our Creator.

Before we encounter God in prayer, we may think we want a better paying job, a bigger house, more worldly recognition. But when we shut ourselves away in the secret place and meet with Jesus, we begin to learn there is nothing sweeter than the sound of his voice, nothing more beautiful than being permitted to worship him.

And when these things start to get a grip on our soul, our intercession for others who need his touch is no longer a duty but a privilege we grasp with joy. To be able to come to the Father through Jesus and ask him to mend broken relationships, to heal the sick and suffering, to reveal himself to those who have not yet met him, becomes the desire of our heart. We don't intercede because we can't think of any other way of helping (all I can do is pray) but because we know our heavenly Father loves those about whom we are concerned and wants to touch their lives.

So, I make no apology for my emphasis to date on developing intimacy with God, but we now need to move beyond that to consider other aspects of prayer. As members of the Royal Priesthood, we have an obligation to stand in the gap on behalf of those who need the Lord's intervention in their lives. However, ability to intercede successfully is dependent on the quality of our personal relationship with Jesus.

Whilst, as God's children we have every right to approach him boldly, we can't expect to rush into the throne room, make our demands, and rush out again. 2 Chronicles 7:14 begins with *if*—a very small but vitally important word. It implies there are conditions we must adhere to in order to have effective prayer lives. Of course, the Lord is very gracious and sometimes answers prayer despite our failure to comply with his ways. But if we want ongoing significant and powerful answers to prayer, we need to take heed of his instructions.

The next phrase is, *my people who are called by my name.* This may seem blindingly obvious, but it is worth some consideration. God was originally talking to Solomon about the people of Israel, the people he had chosen from amongst the nations to be his treasured possession, and to be a light to the world to reveal what he is like. The privilege of having prayers heard and answered by God is dependent on us being his people and being known as such.

This isn't just about being saved, but recognising, as I heard Paul Miller once say that the Lord has paid the price to own us. We no longer have the right of authority over our own lives. We are to become the living sacrifices that Paul urges us to be in Romans 12:1. If our prayers are to have power, then all the forces in the heavenly realms, both good and evil, need to know that we have accepted our place under the authority of our Father.

If my people . . . will humble themselves says God. Humility is *not* part of the fruit of the Spirit (Gal. 5:22-23). On the contrary, it is something we are expected to work on for ourselves. James 4:10 says, *humble yourselves before the Lord.* It takes an act of the will to humble yourself before God. But it is what is required, and it's much more comfortable to humble yourself than to wait for God to bring you to humility against your will, perhaps even through humiliation.

Humility is really no more than recognising our own poverty before Almighty God. That is what worship is about. We cannot truly worship without being humble before God. As we declare his great and awesome power and might, his holiness, perfection, and beauty, his wisdom, justice, and understanding, his compassion and tender care, we cannot help but recognise the vast difference between the Creator and us, his creatures.

Who is in charge of your life, you or your Saviour? Whose will matters most to you, yours or the Lord's? Does your prayer life spring from a desire to receive what you want or to bring his plans to fulfillment?

If my people . . . will pray. Why pray when you can worry? Sometimes prayer is our last resort. We exhaust every other option first. We worry, analyse, discuss, strategise, try a few things. Then when nothing else works, we decide all that is left is prayer, so we turn to the Lord and say, *I've run out of options, please will you intervene?* We need to completely change our direction so that prayer is the first item on the agenda.

Failure to prioritise prayer is an indication that we have not yet learnt the lesson of humility. When prayer isn't our first thought, we are effectively saying to the Lord, *I don't need you. I can find a way to do this on my own.* That is pride, the kind of pride that began the building of the tower at Babel. But 2 Chronicles 7:14 shows us that prayer is essential to God's intervention, and without it, we won't see the changes in the world around us which we long for. Activity is good, but it needs to be preceded by prayer—prayer plus activity equals productivity.

The next condition given is that we seek God's face. This is what this book is primarily about—seeking God's face. So often prayer becomes a matter of seeking God's hand for his blessing. There is nothing wrong with asking the Lord to supply our needs. Indeed, the Lord Jesus taught us to pray for our needs to be met. But seeking God's face, seeking him for who he is, must precede our requests for help.

When we love someone, we enjoy being with them. We want to be around them just for the pleasure of their company and with no ulterior motives. If we seek God's face simply because we think it's a step towards getting our prayers answered, we will fail miserably. If we are in a love relationship with the Lord Jesus, then we should desire to seek his face with all our heart. It is on a foundation of love, not a set of procedures that we will build a prayer life that is productive. It's a hard question to ask ourselves, but one which we should be examining regularly. Am I praying to get my needs met or to seek the face of the Lord? It is vital to do both, but the effectiveness of intercession and supplication will be dependent on the extent to which our prayer life is an expression of our love for God.

I once heard Andrew Wommack say that 95 per cent of our prayer lives should be about seeking the face of God and that only a small proportion of our prayer should be intercession. That is not to diminish the value of praying for our needs or the needs of others, but to emphasise that in order to pray effectively and according to the will of God, we need to spend time in his presence getting to know him and understanding his desires.

When we look at our world, the little bit of it in which we live or the bigger global picture, we see problems. But we only see these problems at a surface level. If we begin to pray about these situations before we have sought God's face, we may actually end up praying contrary to the will of God, even though we have the best of intentions and a desire to see him putting things right.

One significant example which comes to mind is China. For years, missionaries worked to take the Gospel to the Chinese people, and a small church was formed. Suddenly all the missionaries were expelled from the country, and Christians around the world wondered what on earth the Lord was doing in removing the support that this fledgling church so desperately needed. There was genuine concern that under the communist regime, the church would experience such persecution that it might die.

Missionaries waited on the borders praying that they would be allowed back into the country so they could once again minister to these baby Christians. It never happened. Instead the Lord used the persecution to strengthen and establish the church. Now, despite being forced underground, it is possibly the fastest growing national church in the world, and I was told recently, by a man whose parents had been amongst those missionaries in China, that there are now more evangelical Christians there than members of the Communist Party. God's solution was very different from man's.

The purpose of prayer is not to see our desires met, but God's plans fulfilled. Before we start interceding, we need to spend time seeking God's face for his will. That means giving him love, worship, and adoration so that we take our focus off our own desires and recognise his absolute sovereign authority. It means reading scripture for the purpose of understanding his character and his passions. It means having the humility to ask him how we should pray and seeking him for the gift of discernment to see beyond the surface of problems into the heart of what he is working to achieve.

In our journey through this verse, discovering some of the essential conditions for answered prayer, we have now reached the really uncomfortable part—*turn from their wicked ways*. Believers are very happy talking about the dreadful state of society and blaming the godlessness of our culture on the sins of this and previous generations. We bemoan the standards of sexual ethics, the ridicule of Christians in the media, the madness of scientists who want to create human-animal hybrids, the breakdown of family life, and the growing dependence on drugs and alcohol. We want to see change, and we pray for those caught up in sin that *they* would turn from their wicked ways to the Lord Jesus.

But that is not what this verse is talking about, for it is not calling on worldly people to repent but God's own people. It's easy for us to blame others for the state of our nations, but the Lord puts the onus and responsibility on us. In this verse, we are not told to preach repentance. Instead, we ourselves are called to turn away from our own wickedness.

Most of us present a nice, tidy front to our fellow believers on a Sunday morning and Wednesday night. I'm sure I'm not the only married person to have a falling out with their spouse just before going to church, smile my way through the service, and continue with the row in the car on the way home. None of us want other believers, who all appear to have got their act together, to know what we're really like under the surface.

But God knows. He knows when we fail to submit to our husbands or love our wives sacrificially. He knows when we use the phone at work for personal calls. He knows when we waste hours on computer games or surfing the net for images we should not allow ourselves to see; he knows when we gossip or store up hatred in our hearts. He knows when we look on others with judgement and condemnation instead of love and compassion. He knows our righteousness is nothing better than filthy rags.

When Paul wrote Galatians 5:16-26 and listed everything from sexual immorality to drunkenness with idolatry, discord, envy, and other forms of depravity, he knew very well that he was speaking to Christians who, even as believers, were capable of falling into such sin. We, like them, need to be warned to turn away from our wicked ways. We cannot expect God to respond to our prayers for those lost in sin if we are perpetuating sin in our own lives.

The history of revivals shows that any genuine movement of the Spirit of God always begins with a renewed sense of the awfulness of sin and true repentance amongst God's people, usually accompanied by great remorse and weeping. If we want to see others coming to faith and our nations changed, we have to heed the condition that we turn from our own wicked ways.

While it's true that the Lord answers many different kinds of prayer, we see, at the end of this verse, what his priorities are. If we understand this, making God's priorities our own will mean that we pray according to his will. Consequently our prayers will be answered. As we have seen, it is God's people who must consciously turn away from sin. This results in an immediate response from him—he forgives. Before all other answers to prayer, the Lord's desire is to restore the broken Father—child relationship with his sons and daughters. He doesn't hide his face from us any longer than is necessary.

Because of the Fall, we have an innate understanding that if we do something wrong, we must pay the consequences. As a result, many of us find it hard to accept God's forgiveness even when we've truly repented. We feel we deserve punishment, and the tendency is to think that we don't deserve restoration of relationship with God. Like Adam in the Garden, we want to hide from him.

But scripture is very clear. There is no condemnation for those who are in Christ Jesus (Rom. 8:1). He has paid the price, and there is nothing more required of us. As long as we behave as though we deserve condemnation, we are of no use to God. We are doing nobody any favours if we continue to mourn over our sin when the Lord has forgiven us and wants us to go forward. We must not stop at repentance. We must accept forgiveness and move on. This is God's priority for his people.

The healing of God's people from sin and the healing of the nations are often linked in scripture. Healing of the land equates to the coming of the Kingdom. A kingdom is simply a place where a king rules. The Lord Jesus himself said that we should seek first the Kingdom of God and his righteousness (Matt. 6:33). In fact, he makes these things a condition for answered prayer in other areas, thus confirming the priorities we see in 2 Chronicles 7:14.

When the Kingdom of God has become a reality in our personal lives, it can begin to be formed in our families, our communities, and our nations. But we have to do our part. The promise of a healed land is conditional on us doing those things we've been studying in this chapter. Above all, we must actually pray, as Jesus taught us, *Your kingdom come.*

As we've said numerous times before, we should be specific. When Caleb, a man in his eighties, entered the Promised Land, he asked for a mountain. He did not say give me a mountain, but, give me *this* mountain (Josh. 14:12). As we seek to see God's Kingdom and rule established in our nations and in the lives of those around us, we need to start to pray for specific situations and specific people. Under the guidance of the Holy Spirit, we should be praying in the manner of Caleb.

The Lord Jesus told his disciples that their faith could move mountains (Matt. 17:20). Seek God's face and search your heart. He will give you a passion to claim a particular mountain. Perhaps it will be to reach a certain family or neighbourhood with the Good News; perhaps it will be to see ungodly legislation overturned. Perhaps it will be for a reduction of crime in your city.

Whatever it is, the Lord has a specific mountain for you to tackle in prayer. If you make as your priorities, first maintaining your personal relationship with God and secondly praying for your mountain, you will begin to see more fruit in your prayer life.

Exercise

Take 2 Chronicles 7:14 with you into your next prayer time and work your way through it. When praying for people, take time to ask the Lord how you should pray and what you should pray for. Allow the Holy Spirit to prompt you by seeding your mind with ideas. When you begin to pray in this way, you will start to see more answers to your prayers because you will be learning to pray in accordance with the will of God.

CHAPTER 29

Fasting

When you fast . . .—

(Matt. 6:16)

I don't know when I last heard any teaching on fasting. This leaves me with the uncomfortable feeling that for many believers, despite the words of Jesus, fasting is not seen as a vital part of a Christian's prayer life. Of course, if we take the Matthew chapter 6 passage seriously, no one will know when we fast, and this can add to the impression that nobody's doing it. I may be completely wrong about whether or not people are fasting, but I want to bring the subject to your attention because it is a key aspect of prayer.

One of the big mistakes we can make is to think that fasting is somehow a way of twisting God's arm to persuade him to do what we want. On the contrary, the fundamental reason for fasting should be to give glory to God. Worship is a discipline. We do it because God is worthy to be worshipped. We see an example of this in Acts 13:2.

While they were worshipping the Lord and fasting, the Holy Spirit
said, Set apart for me Barnabas and Saul for the work to which I
have called them.

Fasting is an act of worship and needs to be undertaken with discipline
and primarily because the Lord is worthy to receive our fast. Many who have
adopted fasting as part of their prayer lives find it beneficial to fast regularly,
perhaps once a week.

Our first thought at the mention of fasting may be the idea of going without
food for a period of time. This is usually described as the *normal fast*. Often this
is undertaken for a twenty-four-hour period, but simply missing a single meal
would be a fast. I have found it possible to make a three-day fast without any
significant adverse consequences, but a longer fast might require some forward
planning. You cannot expect to carry on your normal routine when you are
not supplying your body with its usual fuel. In any case, I am inclined to think
that you probably need clear direction from the Lord to undertake anything
more than a one day fast, and in doing so, you will probably be asked to spend
significant times in prayer, which would inhibit your normal lifestyle. It is vitally
important to mention here that if you have any kind of medical condition, you
should seek a doctor's advice before undertaking a fast, but for most people,
any health issues should not affect the ability to fast.

Simply going without food is not the only kind of fast. There are many
different types mentioned in scripture. We see Daniel and his friends refraining
from eating certain types of food, and this is sometimes described as a *partial
fast* (Dan. 1:6-16). This type of fast could well be suitable for those for whom a
normal fast is medically problematic. A favourite for some people is to give up
something for Lent, and this is a legitimate fast if it requires a genuine sacrifice
and self-discipline.

There are instances of people going without both food *and* water for a period which we might call a total or *absolute fast* (Acts 9:9, Esther 4:16). I have never undertaken such a fast, and I am absolutely convinced you need a very clear call from the Lord to a total fast. The human body can survive a long time without food but deteriorates very rapidly without water. No one, however healthy, should make a total fast without medical advice.

Fasting from food is not the only kind of fasting described in scripture. For example, Paul indicates in 1 Corinthians 7:3-5 that sexual abstinence for the purpose of devoting ourselves to prayer is a form of fasting. Forsaking any kind of activity can fulfill the function of a fast. Fasting from TV to have more time to pray is something I have found beneficial.

The first and most practical result of fasting is that it frees up time you would have spent eating. This means there is additional time for prayer. Fasting can also help to clarify our own prayer requests. The psalmist says that if we delight in the Lord, he will give us the desire of our hearts (Ps. 37:4). Fasting can be both evidence that we delight in the Lord and proof that what we are seeking God for is truly our heart's desire. If I want to see a particular answer to prayer, is it important enough for me to fast over it?

Finally, fasting can sharpen the spiritual senses. In fasting, we humble ourselves before God, and whilst our stomach may growl loudly, our spirit often becomes more sensitive to the voice of God, making prayer easier.

If you have never fasted, begin by making a partial fast or simply miss one meal. Over a period of months, you can build up to a twenty-four-hour fast. You may feel that you can begin with a daylong fast, but you should not attempt anything longer than that until you have gained some experience.

If you regularly consume caffeine (coffee, tea, energy drinks), or high levels of sugar or junk food on a daily basis, your body is going to suffer withdrawal symptoms from these addictive substances when you fast, the most common problem being headaches. You have a number of options: Allow yourself to consume these things during the fast, live with the effects of withdrawal, or prepare yourself in advance by weaning yourself off them a few days before you fast.

Some people find difficulty in consuming only water during a normal fast. But you should aim to drink plenty of water. If this is a problem, you could try adding some unsweetened fruit juice to your water.

Exercise

Give prayerful consideration to how you might incorporate fasting into your prayer life. If you are unsure what God might be saying to you, try swapping half an hour of some pleasurable activity (reading, watching TV, playing computer games) for an extra half an hour of prayer one day this week. See what happens.

CHAPTER 30

A Cord of Three Strands

Pray for me.

(Eph. 6:19)

Paul repeatedly asked those to whom he was writing to pray for him and for those working alongside him (Col. 4:3, 1 Thess. 5:25, 2 Thess. 3:1). Why is it then that we sometimes find it so difficult to ask for prayer for ourselves or even for our loved ones?

Perhaps we want to deal with the situation in which we find ourselves without seeking extra support. Either we think we should be strong enough in ourselves and not require divine intervention at all or, if we do need some help from God, we want to believe that our own prayers are sufficient, and we don't need the prayers of others. There is a word for this—pride. *I can do all things*, but only through Christ who strengthens me (Phil. 4:13). It is our brothers and sisters who are the body of Christ, and strength comes when we ask them to join in prayer with us for our needs. It is foolishness to think we can do it all on our own.

If the great Apostle to the Gentiles, the writer of more than a quarter of the New Testament, a man who had experienced indescribable visions of glory, could ask for prayer from those he had preached the Gospel to, then surely we can humble ourselves to ask our brothers and sisters in Christ to pray for us in our need.

Battling on alone without sharing our burdens with others is not somehow a badge of greater spirituality. It is not scriptural. The much neglected book of Ecclesiastes has something extremely valuable to teach us about the importance of sharing with one another.

> Though one may be overpowered, two can defend themselves. A cord of three strands is not quickly broken. (Eccles. 4:12)

We know that our enemy the devil is looking for opportunities to pick us off (1 Pet. 5:8). If we stand together with someone else, we are stronger. But we become potentially undefeatable when we stand together in prayer because we involve the Lord as the third strand.

Another factor is fear. We are sometimes afraid to make ourselves vulnerable to one another because we don't want to be hurt or rejected. It is desperately sad that within the family of believers, we sometimes have to be cautious about how much we share and with whom because not everyone is as trustworthy as they should be. If we have been honest with another Christian about a struggle we have faced and sought support and prayer, only to be told how weak we are or to be gossiped about, it becomes so much harder to take the risk to be vulnerable again.

But this is precisely what the devil wants. He wants us to be isolated from one another, to feel that we are alone in our problems, that no one else struggles with the same failures and sins that beset us. The devil knows the power of prayer, and he doesn't want us to have access to the divine power which is made available through prayer. Jesus said that, if we agree with one another in prayer, whatever we ask for will be done (Matt. 18:19).

It should be some comfort to us that even the great Apostle Paul found himself in extremis at times.

> We were crushed and overwhelmed beyond our ability to endure,
> and we thought we would never live through it. (2 Cor. 1:8)

No one is immune to seemingly overwhelming difficulties, even the most spiritual men and women amongst us. Yet you wouldn't always know this by the way some Christian leaders behave. It would be so much more encouraging and comforting if our leaders would sometimes be a little more open about their struggles. But we take greater comfort from the fact that we have fellowship with *the God of all comfort* (2 Cor. 1:3).

It has been said by someone far wiser than me that we only realise that God is all we need when we find that he is all we have. Paul says,

> We stopped relying on ourselves and learned to rely only on God.
> (2 Cor. 1:9)

He and his companions learnt that the Lord was faithful and trustworthy, that he did rescue them from their difficult circumstances. Through these experiences, their faith and confidence in God grew.

Sometimes we look at the challenges faced by our loved ones and feel impotent. As we have observed before, we may even say, *I don't know what else to do but pray*. But Paul recognised the utmost importance of prayer. *You are helping us by praying for us*, he says (verse 11). We should never undervalue the power of prayer. It may be that our simple prayer is the key to resolving the problems faced by those we care about.

For reasons best known to himself, God chooses to act in response to prayer. We can pray that those who are struggling do indeed experience the comfort of the felt presence of Jesus or that they have the strength to stand firm in their troubles. We can pray that the Lord will stir the hearts of those who can help in practical ways or that he will give wisdom, insight, and understanding so that problems can be solved.

I have seen some remarkable answers to prayer over the years, one minor miracle within just five minutes of praying. These answers have all come in response to interceding for others. Intercession has to be founded on a strong relationship with Jesus in order to be really effective. But if all we are doing is glorying in the wonder of his presence and not working with him to meet the needs of others, we are not loving him with all our heart.

> Carry each other's burdens, and in this way you will fulfill the law
> of Christ. (Gal. 6:2)

It is a command of scripture that we bear one another's burdens. There is a saying that a trouble shared is a trouble halved, but that is not the message of the verse above. The implication in Paul's instruction is that we take responsibility for the whole load. Whilst we may not always be able to do this in practical terms, it is something we can do in prayer. When someone shares a need with us, we can take full responsibility for praying about it. In fact, we should pray as though the only thing that will be effective in the situation is our prayer. We should pray as though there is no one else to pray. We should pray as though the only solution is a miracle from God.

The very word *burden* implies something which is difficult to carry alone. That means that it is not an easy thing to get alongside someone and take their load upon ourselves. It may well seem heavy to us too. When interceding for others, we have to be careful we don't simply become anxious on their behalf.

Particularly when praying for loved ones, it is all too easy to become consumed with concern for them in their difficulties. But we are told,

Cast all your anxiety on Him because He cares for you. (1 Pet. 5:7)

This applies to our own concerns, but also to the burdens of others which we have taken up in prayer. Their cares become ours and as we pray we give them to the Lord and leave them with Him. Since we are fulfilling the law of Christ, described in Galatians 6:2, we are taking His yoke upon us which we should find light and easy to bear (Matt. 11:28-30). If the burden seems heavy we should ask ourselves whether we're really praying or just worrying.

One of the greatest gifts you can give someone is your faith. I'm not talking about giving away your faith in evangelism, but praying with faith.

If you believe, you will receive whatever you ask for in prayer. (Matt. 21:22)

There have been times when I have lost hope in a particular situation. I have been unable to believe that God would do the miracle I so desperately needed. I believed God could, but I wasn't sure he would. I couldn't pray with the kind of faith and belief the Lord Jesus was talking about in this passage from Matthew.

I recall one particular occasion when I did not have the faith, but a dear friend did. She continued to pray after I had given up. She also kept telling me that she believed God would do the miracle. I remained skeptical despite her continued encouragement. I cannot tell you how grateful I was to her as well as to the Lord when the answer came and the miracle happened.

It's often easier for us to have faith for someone else than for ourselves. While I struggled to believe for my miracle, I am having no difficulty believing for a miracle for another friend with a desperate problem. On the surface, the situation looks a mess, but as I pray for her, I am seeing small but significant changes which tell me that God is at work.

This faith is exemplified by the friends who carried a young man on his bed to the roof of the house where Jesus was, dug a hole in it, and let him down to set him before the Lord (Mark 2:1-5). We sometimes use the Christian jargon of *lifting someone up* to the Lord in prayer. When I first heard that phrase, I was baffled by it. But here was the reverse—letting someone down before the Lord! No mention is made of the paralysed man's faith, but his friends had the faith in Jesus to carry him there and wreck somebody else's roof. Jesus responded to their faith and their actions.

We need one another, not simply for fellowship, but to stand beside us in prayer when we're struggling to hold up our shield of faith. In the famous *spiritual armour* passage in Ephesians 6:10-20, Paul tells us four times to stand—take your stand, stand your ground, stand, stand firm. Paul borrows metaphors from the practices of the Roman army. Amongst other strategies was the one where they simply stood rank by rank, with their shields together to perform an impenetrable barrier. Each soldier was protected by their own shield but also by those of the soldiers on either side of him. Sometimes all we are capable of is standing. At such times, we need the faith-filled prayers of our brothers and sisters, standing alongside us, locking their shields with ours as the Roman soldiers did, and helping us to stand.

There is another side to this relationship of praying for one another. It has been said that when we pray about something, we should be willing to be the answer to our own prayers. We should also be open to the idea that we can be the answer to other people's prayers. There is a very familiar passage in Matthew in which Jesus talks about prayer. At the end of this, *ask-seek-knock* teaching in Matthew 7:7-11, Jesus says this:

Do to others whatever you would like them to do to you. (Matt. 7:12, NLT)

We know that God uses people to answer prayers. There are countless stories of someone praying for money and receiving it just in time, but no one ever received a physical cheque drawn on the 'Bank of Heaven' and signed by the hand of God. There are numerous practical examples of prayers being answered by individuals responding to the promptings of the Holy Spirit.

The question then arises about what happens to the prayer if the person called on by the Lord to act fails to do so. Could it be that God sometimes gets the blame for unanswered prayer because one of his people didn't have the nerve to step out in faith and do as they were told?

A regular part of our prayer life should be to ask the Lord how we can bless others and seek out opportunities for answering people's prayers. We are, after all, the body of Christ, and he delights to use us.

Exercise

Ask yourself how willing you are to share your burdens with others. If this is something you have been reluctant to do, try to find one thing, no matter how trivial, that you can ask a Christian friend to pray about this week. If you're not aware of any specific needs, simply ask them to pray one of Paul's prayers for you—that you will be filled with joy and peace (Rom. 15:13). If you have a particular struggle at the moment, ask the Lord to guide you to the right person who can support you and stand with you in prayer. A mature believer will consider it a great privilege to be asked to pray for you in this way.

If someone asks you to pray for them, make sure you do two things. Firstly, actually pray. It is all too easy to say you will pray and then forget! Secondly, let them know periodically that you're continuing to do so. From my own experience, it is a great encouragement when someone tells me they're still praying for a situation that isn't yet resolved.

Finally, do for someone what you would like them to do for you. Ask the Lord to show you what you can do to be a part of the answer to another person's prayer.

CHAPTER 31

Unity and Diversity

All the believers were together and had everything in common.

(Acts 2:44)

*I*n the early days of the Christian church, there were no denominations. People were either believers or not. Most of the towns or cities where there were disciples of Jesus had single congregations. There was no picking and choosing which fellowship to belong to. You couldn't fall out with someone and go to another church down the road. Divisions first began to set in when the Gospel reached the Gentiles, and there was sometimes friction with the Jewish believers. But even where this was the case, they were not divided into separate churches.

Today in the West, we have a plethora of Christian denominations, and we have managed to plant all of these and more in cultures around the world where we have sent missionaries. You can visit just about any town or village in Britain and choose where to worship from a choice of congregations: Anglican, Methodist, Baptist, Brethren, Pentecostal, Traditional, Evangelical . . . the list goes on and on. This means that people with a particular theological leaning or a desire to worship in a particular manner can congregate together.

This has its advantages. Where differences between people are minimised, harmony should be greater. For example, someone who practises speaking in tongues will not have to keep justifying their belief within a Pentecostal church but may have a lot of explaining to do within a Methodist congregation. Someone else who prefers a contemplative style of worship may feel at home in a Brethren assembly but completely out of place in a Charismatic fellowship.

So we have the luxury of finding a church we can feel comfortable in, where our theology is not questioned, and our style of worship is considered acceptable. In some ways, this is a positive thing because it fosters acceptance and unity within the group.

However, this also creates problems because it tends to lead towards imbalance. We are in danger of segregating different personality types in different Christian ghettos.

I wonder if Paul could have used his analogy of the body (1 Cor. 12) in many of our modern churches for, it seems to me, that different parts of the body have ended up in different congregations. There are some churches full of exuberant teens-and-twenties, while others soldier on with an average age in the sixties.

Some churches are filled with people whose focus is on evangelism while others are concerned with social justice. Some encourage congregational participation while others limit ministry to a few. Some place scripture and hearing God's Word at the heart of their services while others consider the focus should be on ministering to God in worship.

So the extroverts go to the Pentecostal church, the introverts kneel quietly in the Church of England pews, the scholars pore over scripture in the Brethren assembly and the artistic types feel liberated in Charismatic meetings.

The church body has been carved up into bits and strewn across the community. In many places, there are attempts to get churches of different denominations working together. But they are rarely successful because there is not a complete understanding of one another. There is a natural distrust because we do not realise that apparent differences in emphasis or worship style are simply down to our God-given differences in personality and gifting.

The local church is supposed to contain all the different members of the body—those who are energised by lively worship and those who are refreshed through quiet contemplation, the vitality and enthusiasm of the young together with the wisdom and maturity that come with age, the iconoclasts and the traditionalists, the pastors and the evangelists, the strong and the weak, the babes in Christ and the fathers in the faith.

All of these differences impact the way we pray, whether it be posture, language, or emotional content. Prayer should not be affected in this way, but it is. I feel comfortable kneeling in an Anglican church, but not in my own fellowship where I've never seen anyone else kneel. In a Charismatic service, I may sing in tongues when other people do but would feel uncomfortable doing the same in a Brethren assembly. I am happy reciting the beautiful words of some liturgical prayers which express my heart but would generally only use extempore prayers in my own church.

Perhaps all this simply reflects my own weakness and my lack of integrity before God in my worship, but I'm not so sure. I think all these expressions of prayer have their value and their place. Though if we spend our entire Christian lives in one congregation or denomination, chances are that we will only experience the blessings of some of these modes of prayer and miss out on others.

Exercise

If you get the opportunity to visit a church from a different tradition from your own, perhaps whilst on holiday, or to meet to pray with believers of other denominations, why not take the risk and step out of your comfort zone. You can start to knit the body back together and, while you gain a deeper understanding of other brothers and sisters, you might even discover new ways of praying which bring you closer to God.

CHAPTER 32

The Fifth Dimension

> Praise be to the God and Father of our Lord Jesus Christ, who has blessed us in the heavenly realms with every spiritual blessing in Christ.
>
> (Eph. 1:3)

I enjoy the sci-fi genre of literature. Though I rarely read such books these days, I am known occasionally to sit in front of the TV and watch *Star Trek*. One of the recurring concepts in these stories is that of beings who live in an alternate dimension, beyond our *space-time continuum*. Often these characters are portrayed as having godlike qualities—being eternally existent, having exceptional powers, and so on.

As human beings, we are firmly grounded in the three dimensions of space. Our bodies are designed with senses to take in information about the physical world around us and to move us through those dimensions. We also have an awareness of the passage of time but have no choice about the direction and rate of travel through this fourth dimension.

Scripture teaches us that there is also a fifth dimension of which most people these days are unaware. The Bible calls this dimension *the heavenly realms*. It is the dimension of the spirit, and it is the place where we encounter God. In many societies around the world, the existence of this dimension is a powerful reality, but in the West, we have become so obsessed with material things that we have largely lost our sense of the spiritual.

Paul was acutely aware of the existence of *the heavenly realms*. In Ephesians, he mentions them five times, and on each occasion, he teaches us something about this world of the spirit that we need to understand if we are to have effective and powerful prayer lives.

The first thing which Paul tells us in Ephesians 1:3 is that the heavenly realms are where we are blessed. He then goes on, through the next eleven verses, describing some of these blessings in quite extravagant terms. Words such as freely given, riches, lavished, and pleasure indicate an abundance of blessing which is ours *in Christ*. When we comprehend the enormity of what we have in Christ, our identity in him, it transforms the way we pray. If we know that we are chosen, adopted, and forgiven, truly know it, we will be bold to enter into prayer, not timid or anxious.

In Verse 20 of chapter 1, Paul tells us that Christ is seated in the heavenly realms at the right hand of God. From this, we can see that the heavenly realms are the place where both the Lord Jesus and our Father dwell. This is why Jesus told the woman at the well that those who worship God should do so in spirit and in truth (John 4:24). Worship which involves only body and soul is inferior worship. We are created with a spirit, and that is the part of our being which communes with God. Our physical bodies and our souls (mind, will, and emotions) may well be involved when we worship, but it is our spirit which embraces God. Jesus told us that he is *the Truth* (John 14:6). It is because we are *in Christ*, who himself is seated at God's right hand in the spiritual dimension, that we are able to offer worship in spirit and in truth.

But it is not only Christ who is seated in the heavenly realms, for in Ephesians 2:5 we are told that God has raised us up to that same position in Christ. We too are seated in the heavenly realms. We have intimate access to the Father through being in Christ. When we worship, when we pray, we do so not from a position of mortals confined to time and space but from the very privileged place at the heart of the throne room of heaven. There need be no concern about whether our prayers are reaching heaven or bouncing back to us from the ceiling above. We do not pray from a distance and wonder whether the message gets through. In the spiritual dimension, we are so close to God that we can whisper and be heard. Sometimes we hear him in our spirit whisper a reply.

In Ephesians 3:10, Paul introduces the concept of *rulers and authorities* who inhabit the heavenly realms. Here he says that one of the Lord's purposes for the church is to reveal what he is like to other spiritual forces. It is not entirely clear here whether Paul is talking about angels or demons, but either way what is clear is that who we are and how we live is not intended simply to be a witness to the human beings around us but also to those beings who are part of the spiritual or heavenly realms.

But in Ephesians 6:12, part of that great treatise on spiritual warfare, Paul goes on to talk about the spiritual beings in the heavenly realms against whom we struggle. These clearly are forces of evil who exist in the same dimension as God and our own spirits. Some believers find it difficult to believe that the devil can exist in the presence of God, but the account of Job gives us a very clear picture of two audiences Satan has with the Lord (Job 1:6-12). From reading elsewhere, we know that there are degrees of heaven.

> I know a man in Christ who fourteen years ago was caught up to the third heaven. Whether it was in the body or out of the body I do not know. God knows. (2 Cor. 12:2)

Precisely who is permitted to enter different degrees of heaven is not clear. What is clear is that there is a spiritual dimension in which God, humanity, and the forces of evil may interact.

Our physical bodies have to deal with the realities of the material world and our relationship with it, so it's very easy to make that the focus of our lives and forget that part of us lives permanently in the presence of God and other spiritual beings in heavenly realms. If we are to have a *successful* Christian life, we need to develop our sensitivity to what is happening in the spiritual dimension. This can only be done by exercising our spirits through communion and fellowship with God in prayer.

Exercise

Ask the Lord to help you *see* spiritually and to understand your relationship with the heavenly realms.

CHAPTER 33

Wrestling Prayer

I do not think (the devil) minds our praying about things if we leave it at that. What he minds, and opposes steadily, is the prayer that prays on until it is prayed through, assured of the answer.

(Mary Warburton Booth)

Oh, men and women, pray through; pray through! Do not just begin to pray and pray a little while and throw up your hands and quit; but pray and pray and pray until God rends the heavens and comes down.

(RA Torrey)

*I*f there is one aspect of prayer which has been almost completely neglected by the modern church, it is that of *wrestling prayer* or *praying through*. In fact in most places where I've mentioned it, I have been met by blank expressions. To learn about it myself, I have largely had to get myself mentored by the old heroes of the faith through writings which are decades, even hundreds of years old. And yet, this type of prayer is taught in scripture.

I have already alluded to an example in the chapter *Take Your Time*. There we saw how Abraham prayed for the residents of Sodom and kept praying until God ended the conversation. Now I want to expand our understanding of this principle.

What Abraham was doing was wrestling with God in prayer. Jacob wrestled with God, but it was to receive a blessing for himself (Gen. 32:22-32). When Abraham wrestled with God, it was on behalf of others. Both are valid—we do neither.

It has become the accepted teaching in many parts of the church that praying in faith means asking God for something once and then trusting him for the answer. This generally leads to three possible outcomes. First, the prayer is answered, and we rejoice. Second, the prayer is not answered, and we accept that God is saying *no*. Third, the prayer is unanswered, and we blame ourselves for not having enough faith. This can be a very unsatisfying way of praying. Answers that come easily tend to lead only to shallow rejoicing while answers which don't come at all tend to lessen our faith. This is a kind of weak, faint copy of prayer as taught in the Bible, prayer that presses through to the answer. Jesus taught about persistent prayer in the parable of the friend asking for bread at midnight (Luke 11:5-8). He followed that up with this statement as given in Luke 11:9-10:

> So I say to you: Ask and it will be given to you; seek and you will find; knock and the door will be opened to you. For everyone who asks receives; the one who seeks finds; and to the one who knocks, the door will be opened.

In our English translations, we miss something very important in these verses. The form of the words *ask*, *seek*, and *knock* is a continuous form. In other words, Jesus is saying, 'Ask and keep asking, seek and keep seeking, knock and keep knocking.' As George Muller has said:

It is not enough for the believer to begin to pray, nor to pray correctly; nor is it enough to continue for a time to pray. We must patiently, believingly continue in prayer until we obtain an answer. Further, we have not only to continue in prayer until the end, but we have also to believe that God does hear us and will answer our prayers. Most frequently we fail in not continuing in prayer until the blessing is obtained, and in not expecting the blessing.

Let's start looking at this in practical terms, and I will give some real life examples so that we understand exactly what we're talking about. I'll begin with my first experience of praying through.

I was spending a short time with an internationally known outreach ministry, and we were spending a few weeks working in a deprived area of one of Britain's largest cities. In particular, we were getting to know, and share the Gospel with, some of the key people in that community. One evening, as we were praying, one of the team, I'll call her, Margaret, began to sense the need to pray for a particular woman who ran the community centre. We all began to pray for this woman that Margaret would have an opportunity to share the Gospel with her and that she would be saved. We must have prayed all around this issue for about an hour, until Margaret said that she felt a breakthrough in her spirit and believed that the prayer was answered. The following day, she did indeed get the opportunity to speak to this community leader who came to faith immediately.

Most recently, a dear Christian friend was diagnosed with cancer. The whole church was praying for and with her at every opportunity, but one evening, as I began to pray for her in the usual way, I sensed that God wanted to take hold of that time of prayer and that I had to keep praying and praying for her. About forty-five minutes later, I had a peaceful sense that everything was going to be all right. As I write, she looks completely well, and no one would know there was anything wrong with her. She continues to have chemotherapy but with none of the usual side effects, and her prognosis is good. Now I am not claiming any special achievement here for myself. Our church has brought an orchestra of prayer to the Lord for my friend, and one of the instruments participating in the symphony was that response to the prompting of the Holy Spirit to pray through. Others have been given the task to pray in different ways. Together we asked, sought, and knocked, and God has graciously answered. Interestingly, my friend says that this episode has encouraged her to persevere in prayer for others too and to grow in her understanding of the faithfulness of God.

Now I can see the blank expression on someone's face when, in order to encourage them, I told them I had prayed for them for half an hour. They couldn't imagine what on earth I had been saying to the Lord for that length of time. Actually, the periods of time I have been using to illustrate this idea are quite short in the scheme of things. Praying through a particular issue may take much longer than that. There are times when people are called to spend whole nights in prayer. At other times, they may be required to pray faithfully, every day, for many years. But God is gracious as always and teaches us in little steps, so it's unlikely your first experience of praying through will be to spend three or four hours on your knees weeping!

But even if you only spend fifteen minutes praying through one issue, what do you fill that time with? Certainly not with repeating the same words over and over again in vain repetition (Matt. 6:7).

> It is the habit of faith, when she is praying, to use pleas. Mere prayer sayers, who do not pray at all, forget to argue with God; but those who prevail bring forth their reasons and their strong arguments. (Charles H. Spurgeon)

Children are very good at this. At least, they are until they are taught not to nag. Every parent knows the wearing down effect of a child on a mission to get what they want. They ask, they plead, they bargain, they reason, they may even weep and wail. You are left in no doubt that they passionately desire what they are asking for. The question is, when we pray, does God get the impression we are desperate for him to work or that we don't really care, that we just thought we would run the idea by him to see if he might help out?

What are we saying to God when we pray these passing prayers? I don't believe you are powerful enough? I don't believe you love me enough? I don't believe you care about that person enough? I don't believe you keep your word? Would you dare to say any of these things to God? Why then would you dare to be what Spurgeon calls, *mere prayer sayers?*

We need to learn to plead with God and not simply recite our requests as happens in most church prayer times these days. We need to become childlike in our praying. That does not mean we are only to use simple words and brief sentences. No, we are to ask as those children ask who really do want something.

We need to remind the Lord of what he's said in his Word. Quote him chapter and verse. 'My friend is having sleepless nights, but it says in your word that the Lord gives sleep to his beloved and she is your child. You said you would do it, so please will you give her sleep tonight.'

We need to pray with passion. 'She is my friend and I care about her, and I can see what all this sleeplessness is doing to her. If I were in the position to do something about it, I would give her sleep.'

We need to reason with God. 'When she can't sleep, she gets headaches, and then she can't care for her family properly. She's in pain. She gets depressed. She's too tired to read her Bible, and her devotional times are affected. She can't do all those things you've called her to do.'

We need to tell God about the impact this is having on his reputation. 'Lord, other people see this, and they say you don't answer prayer, that you don't care about your people, or even that you don't exist. My friend is struggling to be a good witness. She feels she is letting down her unsaved husband and her secular employer, and they are getting a bad impression of what Christians are like.'

Now you might be about to tell me that God knows all this, and he does. But he wants to hear it from you. He wants *you* to know that what you are asking for does actually matter to you. And if it genuinely does matter, then you *will* pray like this because it is a genuine desire of your heart. What does God do with the desires of our hearts? We have already seen that he gives them to us. But we must pray on until we sense in our spirit that he has given his answer.

Exercise

Ask God to teach you specifically about praying through and ask him to give you a particular person or situation to pray for in this way. Make sure you record it in your prayer diary and begin praying.

CHAPTER 34

Attacks on Prayer

Depend upon it, if you are bent on prayer, the devil will not leave you alone. He will *molest you*, tantalise you, block you, and will surely find some hindrances, big or little or both. And we sometimes fail because we are ignorant of his devices.

(Mary Warburton Booth)

It is undoubtedly true that the less you trouble the devil, the less interested he will be in you. We only have to look at the lives of the great men and women of God to see how true that is. Beginning with Stephen, the first martyr, through the Apostle Paul and every generation right up to the modern day, Christians who make a difference for the kingdom are the ones who suffer. This is as much true of prayers as it is of missionaries and evangelists.

As Mary Warburton Booth indicates, it's not so much the attacks that are the problem as our failure to recognise them as such. Paul told the Corinthians, *We are not unaware of his schemes* (2 Cor. 2:11). Neither should *we* be. Earlier on in this book, we looked at the minor distractions that can interfere with our praying and how to deal with these. But now we are getting into the deeper reaches of prayer we need to understand a little more about the devil's tactics.

If you start to get a reputation in the heavenly realms for being a prayer, the first tactic of the devil will be to find ways to prevent you from praying. He will try to rob you of your time by finding other things to fill it.

I remember a time when I had made a commitment to step up to the next level with my prayer life. In fact, it was the very day that I planned to begin a new regime of prayer and had reorganized my schedule to be able to do that. My husband and I had to visit the tax office to sort out some problems, and when we got home, we found numerous messages on the phone telling us that our eldest son, who was twelve at the time, had broken his leg during a game of football at school. The rest of that day was spent dashing between home and hospital and arranging for friends to care for our other two sons. It wasn't only that day that became a wipe-out. He was in hospital for four days while they tried to find an operating slot to put a pin in his leg. When he came home, he could do nothing for himself. His bed had to be moved downstairs to the dining room, disrupting our whole family life. We had to have tutors in to help him with schoolwork, which meant I felt obliged to do more housework than I would normally do! It was months before he was able to go back to school, and our lives returned to what passes as normal in the Scotson family.

It was easy to spot the devil's hand in this particular set of circumstances. Everything about it was bad from the pain my son was in, through the difficulty the doctors had in finding a slot to do the surgery, to the ongoing disruption of our lives.

It's not always so obvious that the devil is stealing our time. The good, they say, is the enemy of the best, and one thing the devil does is to tempt us with wonderful opportunities to do something good, which we feel we have to accept. To do otherwise could seem mean, lazy, or even *unspiritual*. If I stay late at a home group meeting discussing the importance of prayer and then struggle to get up in time to have my devotions before going to work, I may look more spiritual to my friends, but my relationship with God won't be so great the following day, and I may be unprepared for the opportunities he brings across my path. The pressure on Christians to *do* things is enormous—come to all the services, the home group, the prayer meeting; get involved with the youth work, the outreach programme, the worship group. By the time you've done all the things expected of you, you are exhausted and cannot give your best to your devotional times. The devil loves that.

All these activities are good, but they're unlikely to all be good for you. Learn to say *no* sometimes, and don't let other Christians use emotional blackmail to persuade you to do something which you know you don't have peace about. In fact, if you say yes, you may be depriving someone else of an opportunity to develop their own ministry. An old adage in the church is *one person, one ministry*. There is a lot to be said for finding your niche and sticking to it. Just because a job needs doing, it doesn't necessarily need doing by you.

A millionaire acquaintance of mine has the practice of replying to every request of him for his time by saying, 'I'm sorry, I'm not available, but if things should change, I'll get back to you.' It's gentler than a straight *no*, and it gives him breathing space to consider whether or not he should accept the invitation.

We have to learn to distinguish between the important and the urgent. Getting to the hospital when my son broke his leg was both urgent and important. But a lot of the claims on our time are urgent but not important or important but not urgent. Here are a couple of possible scenarios.

An elderly lady who can't get to the local Christian bookshop asks me to get her a copy of a book that I mentioned during a sermon. Obviously that's important, but it's not so urgent that I have to reschedule all my plans for tomorrow in order to go straight out and get it. I won't be seeing her again until next Sunday, and I will be in the area of the bookshop on Thursday, so I can easily do it then without trying to cram it into one of my busiest days and neglecting the time I'd planned to spend in prayer.

I have arranged to visit a member of the church who is clinically depressed. No one else in the fellowship is aware of the personal struggles she is facing. But a couple of hours before I'm due to visit her, I get a call from the leader of the evangelism team. The woman who was supposed to go with him to talk to a couple about coming to church has had to cancel, could I stand in? This is urgent—the appointment is made and needs to be kept. It's clearly important too, but is it important for me? I know that there are other people he could ask to go with him and that it wouldn't be a disaster if he ended up having to go alone. I also know that my depressed friend would be devastated if I didn't visit and pray with her as I had committed to do. For me, the more important thing to do is keep my existing promise, even though I cannot give a good reason to the evangelist because of the confidentiality of the situation.

Judging whether something is important or urgent can be very tricky, but learning to listen to the prompting of the Holy Spirit will make it easier. If it's neither urgent nor important, stay clear of it unless you sense that it really is something God wants you to do.

The devil will also try to disrupt you with health problems. Not all sickness is a direct attack from him. If you drink gallons of coffee all week at work and then have a long lie in on Saturday morning, you are likely to wake up with a caffeine withdrawal headache. That's entirely your responsibility.

I have learnt how to tell quite quickly whether ill health is genuine or an attack from the devil to prevent me from praying. It really is quite simple. If at all possible, ignore the problem and carry on. Let me give you an example. There have been several times when I have woken up on a Sunday morning with the kind of headache that could keep me in bed. However, when I've pressed on and gone to church, the headache has lifted completely. Clearly, someone didn't want me to go and worship God with my Christian family, but they gave up their attack when I showed them they weren't going to win.

Worry can be another prayer killer. I used to spend hours some nights lying awake, worrying about one thing or another—usually money and paying the bills. The devil knows our weak points, and the things which cause you great concern may be quite different. Of course if you're awake half the night worrying, you won't be in a great place for concentrated prayer in the morning.

One day, I realised something which radically changed my life—worrying doesn't change anything. I decided that I was going to give up my addiction to worry. Now if I can do something about the problem, I do it. If there's nothing I can do, then I cast my cares on Jesus. And in the middle of the night, there is nothing I can do, so I simply pray, *Lord, I trust you with this*, and go back to sleep. On the occasions when that seems difficult, I spend some time praying for others. The devil stops pestering me, and I soon drift off again. There's a very simple principle here, which is taking captive every thought (2 Cor. 10:5), and it really does work.

Probably the toughest attack to face is the misunderstanding or rejection that may come from others, particularly family and friends. The devil will try to stop us praying by making us disillusioned or depressed, and one of the ways he does this is to try to cause a breakdown in precious relationships. As you travel higher into the mountains of prayer, you will begin to find that conflict arises in your personal life. This may be directly because people see you changing, and they don't want you to change. Or it may simply be that the devil instigates breakdowns in communication. You may find yourself misunderstood, rejected, misrepresented, or even lied about. Take courage—the Lord Jesus went through exactly the same thing.

I confess that when this first started to happen to me, I handled it very badly. In trying to defend myself, I increased the friction in the very relationships I was trying to restore. This is where we have to follow Jesus so closely and imitate his example. He told us we would have to take up our cross daily, and the only place you're going if you're carrying a cross is to death. We need to die to self, to remain silent before our accusers as he did and trust God to vindicate us in his own time (Ps. 35:24, 135:14). That is an incredibly hard thing to do, but anything else plays into the devil's hand. God simply requires us to love our enemies and pray for our persecutors (Matt. 5:44). Don't allow these kinds of upsets to unsettle your prayer life, instead use them to fire up your prayers to a greater intensity.

I am sure that the devil's devices to stop us praying are many and varied, and there is no way to cover them all here. But I hope I've given you enough examples to give you some insight into his tactics so that you become aware of when he is attempting to interfere with your prayer life.

Exercise

Consider the events of the past week. Are there times when you'd intended to pray but didn't? Why was this? What could you do to prevent the same thing happening again?

CHAPTER 35

Praying Through Grief

In this you greatly rejoice, though now for a little while you may have
had to suffer grief in all kinds of trials.

(1 Pet. 1:6)

A few months ago, a beloved family member died after a very short and
sudden illness. Three days after her funeral, the husband of one of my dearest
friends passed away. Within two months, another two friends lost loved ones
quite unexpectedly. So many people I care about are experiencing grief, and in
the heart of such a distressing emotion, it is hard to understand how the Apostle
Peter can talk about grief and rejoicing in the same sentence.

But Peter isn't just teaching that we should rejoice when we are grieving.
He actually says that despite their grief, the believers to whom he was writing
were rejoicing. This isn't simply theology or spiritual theory. These ordinary
men and women were actually rejoicing and grieving at the same time. Even
more, they were rejoicing greatly. In the midst of grief, it is hard to see how two
such contrasting emotions can exist together. Yet these Christians had found
a way, not to suppress their grief, but to balance it with joy.

We have to be so careful here. I have heard Christians say to grieving people, *You shouldn't be grieving, God should be enough for you,* and they quote Paul who commanded the Philippians to *rejoice in the Lord always* (Phil. 4:4). But he wasn't asking them to pretend that everything was wonderful when it wasn't. Pretending to be happy when you're feeling broken hearted won't help you; it will just delay the grieving process.

Let's just take a bit of time here to think about human connectedness and why losing a loved one is so painful. When God made Adam, he was designed to have fellowship with God, to be in relationship with him. But that wasn't enough. God himself said,

It is not good for the man to be alone (Gen. 2:18).

God saying that he alone was not enough for Adam? To some people, this sounds like heresy, and perhaps it would be if it was not for the fact that it was God who said it. But the scripture is clear that there was no suitable companion for Adam until God made Eve. As the account progresses, we find that this is not just a one-off relationship. For all time, men and women will join with one another in a one-flesh relationship—two people become one.

We can learn two things from this. Firstly, human beings were created with a need to be in relationship with other human beings, not only with God. Secondly, the intimate relationship between one man and one woman is a special case of this because there is more than simple companionship involved.

But there is another vital factor to be considered, and that is that these relationships were intended to be eternal relationships—we were never supposed to be separated by death. Death is the result of the sin in the garden (Gen. 2:17). We were supposed to be able to live in relationship from the day of our birth through the rest of eternity. But the impostor, death, has cheated us of that. So now, when we are separated from a loved one through death, we feel as though part of our very selves has been torn away. And this is especially true for husbands and wives who have not simply been companions but one flesh.

Grief, even intense grief is normal and a healthy response to the tearing apart of what are supposed to be eternal relationships. Let's not forget that Jesus himself wept at the tomb of Lazarus. I have heard all sorts of explanations for this. My gut feeling is that Jesus wept for the universal tragedy of the pain of separation through death, a separation none of us were designed to cope with. But we can be encouraged that this wrenching apart is temporary, not permanent. And yet, we still have to grapple with this rejoicing issue.

So how do we do this? How do we balance grief and joy, accepting both as valid emotions? In 1 Peter 1:3-5, we see what it is that Peter's audience were rejoicing in—their salvation. Peter himself explodes into praise for new birth, for Christ's resurrection, for our coming perfect inheritance, and the powerful protection we have from God.

Let me ask, have we lost the wonder of what it means to be saved and all the blessings which accrue from that? When was the last time you felt excited about all that God's done for you? When did you last *greatly rejoice* in your salvation? We need to develop a practice of regularly reminding ourselves of all we have in Christ. This is one of the reasons the Lord Jesus instituted the memorial practice of communion—to remember him (Luke 22:19).

We have talked already about allowing other people to pray for us in our need. This is especially true when we are grieving. We need a companion who will walk through the valley of the shadow of death with us, someone who will weep with us (Rom. 12:15) and not judge us for our raw emotions, and who, above all, will take time to pray with us and for us. There will be the practical friends who will shop, prepare meals, give lifts, and help to ease us back into the routine of living. These friends who care for our physical and emotional needs help to carry us through the dark times, to relieve us of the practical burdens. But we also need to be carried in prayer. We need someone who will pray for and with us when we have no words of our own. We need the comfort of hearing a friend who loves us, bringing our situation before the throne of grace. We need to know that we are being prayed for day by day. And we need someone who will lift from us, temporarily, the responsibility of maintaining our spiritual life until the joy of our salvation returns.

Let me also say a little more about shadows. In a sense, as mortal beings, we all constantly live in the valley of the shadow of death whether we are aware of it or not. I wrote a poem called *In The Shadow* several years ago when I was staring into to the face of a desire to give up living. I've included it in the Devotions section.

What I discovered at that point in my life was that there is a very close relationship between the horror of the valley of the shadow of death and the comfort of being in the shadow of God's wings.

In Psalm 61:4, David recalls his history with God, and his current difficulties prompt him to say that he longs to be in the shadow of God's wings. It is clearly a place of great comfort to him. There are a surprising number of references in the Bible to the shadow of God's wings, and each of them teaches us something, a little different.

The first mention is in Ruth 2:12 when Boaz pronounces a blessing over her. Ruth, he says, has come to *take* refuge under the shadow of God's wings. This is important because we need to understand that we have a choice about whether or not to occupy this place of safety and comfort. We don't just find ourselves there in difficult times; we have to make the journey, as Ruth did. We have to seek out and take up the offer of sanctuary.

The Psalms have many references to the shadow of God's wings. In Psalm 17:8, we learn that it is a place where we can *hide from our enemies*. Psalm 36:7 teaches us that we don't have to be anyone special to be able to find this place of refuge—it is *for both high and low*. In other words, it doesn't matter whether you are in church leadership or a brand new believer. You don't have to know your Bible inside out, but it doesn't matter if you do. You can be wealthy or surviving on state benefits. You can be a reasoning adult or an innocent child. The shadow of God's wings is available to you.

Psalm 57:1 shows us that we can stay in this place of comfort *until the disaster is past.* There is good news, and there is bad news in this verse. The bad news is that, just as Jesus told us, we are going to go through very difficult times (John 16:33). The good news is that we can stay in the shadow of God's wings throughout those times. It isn't just a temporary place of respite where we can go to lick our wounds before going out and facing the attacks again. God doesn't tell us to stop running away and pull ourselves together. He makes this place of safety available to us for as long as we need it.

Psalm 63:7 talks about *singing* in the shadow of God's wings. It is a remarkable truth that even in our times of despair, when we draw close to God, we have something to sing about, something to worship him for. In the shadow of his wings, we are close to his heart, surrounded by his love. In Psalm 91:4, we are reminded that under God's wings, we are *covered* by his feathers. We are not simply in the shadow of his wings—he wraps them around us, drawing us close to himself.

Finally, we come to what Jesus said while looking over Jerusalem:

> Jerusalem, Jerusalem, you who kill the prophets and stone those sent
> to you, how often I have longed to gather your children together, as
> a hen gathers her chicks under her wings, and you were not willing.
> (Matt 23:37)

Here is perhaps the most wonderful truth of all—he loves us so much that *he longs* to draw us into this most intimate place of the shadow of his wings. These words are spoken over those who have most firmly rejected God and his word to them. Even those who have turned away from the Lord can return and find refuge in him.

Exercise

Spend some time praising God for as many aspects of salvation as you can think of. If that's a struggle pray with David, *restore to me the joy of your salvation* (Ps. 51:12).

CHAPTER 36

Humility

Oh, the matchless love of God! Truly if there is any glory, it must all be the Lord's. If there is any virtue, it is the result of grace. If there is anything whatsoever which lifts us above the Devil himself, it is the work of the divine Spirit, to whom be glory!

(CH Spurgeon)

*A*s we come to the end of our study on growing our prayer lives, there is one vital last thought I want to share with you. As we get closer to God and begin to experience new depths of intimacy with Jesus, we may look around us and think that we are somehow doing better than others. There may be a temptation towards arrogance or even a judgmental attitude.

We must constantly remind ourselves that any blessings we receive are all by the grace of God, that we have done nothing to earn such blessings and that he could choose to remove them at any time. We must remain humble.

It is notable that humility is not part of the fruit of the Spirit (Gal. 5:22-23). It is something God expects us to work on for ourselves. We are to humble ourselves (Jas. 4:10, 1 Pet. 5:6), an injunction which is always followed by a promise that God will *lift you up*.

Since God objects to pride, you can be sure that a lack of humility will seriously impact your prayer life and deal a heavy blow to your intimacy with him.

> All of you, clothe yourselves with humility towards one another,
> because, God opposes the proud but gives grace to the humble. (1
> Pet. 5:5)

Don't become someone whom God opposes—he will humble the arrogant. He may even allow them to be humiliated if that is what it takes. Why is this? Because,

> I am the Lord; that is my name! I will not give my glory to another
> or my praise to idols. (Is. 42:8)

It is not down to our self-discipline, the length of time we give to prayer, or our righteous lifestyle that we may have breathtaking encounters with God. It is *all* due to his grace and mercy. Yes, he does reward those who diligently and earnestly seek him. But when our motives slip from simply wanting to know him to wanting to boast about our closeness to him, we attempt to take his glory for ourselves. That is something he will not stand for.

But sometimes, the blessings are so great that it is almost impossible for us to maintain our humility. Listen to Paul's experience.

To keep me from becoming conceited because of these surpassingly great revelations, there was given me a thorn in my flesh, a messenger of Satan, to torment me. Three times I pleaded with the Lord to take it away from me. But He said to me, My grace is sufficient for you, for my power is made perfect in weakness. Therefore I will boast all the more gladly about my weaknesses, so that Christ's power may rest on me. That is why, for Christ's sake, I delight in weaknesses, in insults, in hardships, in persecutions, in difficulties. For when I am weak, then I am strong. (2 Cor. 12:7-10)

If we are not able to humble ourselves, God will do it for us. And we will learn that all the afflictions we may suffer are nothing *compared to the surpassing greatness of knowing Christ Jesus my Lord, for whose sake I have lost all things. I consider them rubbish, that I may gain Christ* (Phil. 3:8).

Exercise

Read Psalm 139 and pray earnestly with the psalmist,

Search me, O God, and know my heart; test me and know my anxious thoughts. See if there is any offensive way in me, and lead me in the way everlasting.

DEVOTIONS

JESUS, I LONG TO SEE YOUR FACE

(A Hymn of Devotion)

Jesus, I long to see your face,
To gaze into your eyes,
To glimpse the beauty of your grace,
And claim at last my prize.

I want to bow before your throne,
The shimm'ring crystal see,
To join with thousand, thousand tongues,
In adoration sing.

It is my heart's desire, oh Lord,
To sing the praise you're due,
To fall upon my face, my God,
Give all my love to you.

You are the fairest of them all,
Your name, perfume poured out.
You are the Lover of my soul,
I would not live without.

I cannot give what you deserve,
While to this flesh confined,
But I will offer all I have,
Of heart and strength and mind.

(may be sung to the hymn tune LYDIA or CRIMOND)

A Love Letter to Jesus

Dear Lord Jesus, I love you,

I thank you for the way you have shown your love to me. You stepped down from heavenly majesty into grubby humanity. You exchanged the glory of being worshipped by all the hosts of heaven to be worshipped by sin-riddled, hurting, and confused people. In your absolute purity, you allowed yourself to be touched by lepers and kissed by prostitutes. You showed absolute compassion to the oppressed and raged at those who oppressed them. You became love incarnate, and those who knew they needed love opened their hearts to you.

But then, you carried out the most loving act ever witnessed in this world—you gave yourself to us completely and submitted yourself to be brutally murdered. We often say that you gave yourself *for* us, and it is true theologically because your sacrifice has paid the price for us to be reunited with the Father. But you also gave yourself *to* us as utterly as it is possible to give. Because of what you did, we can now have you living within us, closer to us than our own breath, loving us from the inside—something which no human being can ever do for us.

Lord Jesus, I thank you that you love me completely, that your love for me will never fail. Your love cannot grow because you are love, but my understanding and appreciation of your love can grow. Please help me to love you more and more each day and give you the worship which you deserve.

Amen

IN THE SHADOW

A Psalm for the Suffering
(Ps. 23:4, Ps. 17:8)

The gorge of shadows in my mind
With death's voice stalking me,
No hope to leave the valley floor
For lacerating scree.
The only path is through the vale
Of tears and lightless days,
Stumbling through the rocks, despair
Leans on a staff of praise
And staggers on with faintest faith
Shutting out the grief which stings
'Til shadows of this hell become
The shadow of your wings.'

And here I rest to feel your warmth
Caress my mind with peace
And salve my tattered, bleeding soul
'Til all my weeping cease.'

GRACE UPON GRACE

A Story of Repentance

The silent night with thoughts that tempt
Draws me towards my failing sin.
Yet I, for endless anguished days,
Resist the cries from deep within
To fall.

Determination weakens now.
My strength is gone, my spirit fails.
With every beat of pounding heart
I hammer in those dreadful nails
Myself.

In desolate grief beside the tomb
I rend my broken, aching soul,
In desperation crying out
For One alone can make me whole,
Again.

And then the radiance of his gaze,
Which turns to flesh the hardest stones,
Touches me with exquisite love.
At last I hear his tender tones:
'Enough!'

Prostrate I fall to worship him,
Forgetting all my tortured fears.
I wash those precious bloodstained feet.
With reverent penitential tears.
'Grace upon grace—
My Lord!'

PRAYER OF REPENTANCE

*L*ord Jesus, when I examine my life, I see that I have fallen short of your perfection and your holiness. I am morally bankrupt before you as I have no way of making myself perfect. I owe you a debt because I have failed to live as you want me to live. I cannot pay that debt because I cannot change myself. I believe you have paid the price for me by dying on the cross and taking all the punishment due to me. I believe you conquered death and are alive today. I repent for my sins; I turn away from them and towards you. Please forgive me. You gave your life for me, and I give my life to you, to live for you and not myself, to do your will and not mine. Please fill me with your Holy Spirit and teach me how to live for you.

Amen.

No Compromise

*Y*ou will need to take some time to think through this devotion. Do not rush it. Prepare yourself by getting pen, paper, and matches!

Lord Jesus, I know that you are perfect and utterly holy. I know that you love me, and you want me to be a part of your perfect bride. But when I look inside my heart and consider the thoughts I sometimes allow to take root in my mind, I know that I am very far from perfect. I know that there are things in me which are offensive to you. I know that I enjoy sin. I know that I seek to satisfy my desires apart from you, and that means I am as much guilty of adultery as any unfaithful spouse.

My precious Saviour, I know that you love me, that your heart is always to forgive me when I turn in repentance towards you. Please show me the depths of my depravity; please give me an utter hatred for sin. Please forgive me for my compromise and for pretending that I can get away with a little bit of sin as long as it's not too bad. Please help me to be truly repentant, to live a life of repentance, to run from even the potential of sin.

Lord Jesus, I thank you, for you have paid the price, suffered the consequences of all my sin on my behalf. You gave everything to bear all my sin; I want to give everything I have to live with a hatred for sin and a desire for perfect holiness. I want to live a life of no compromise with sin. Please help me because I cannot do this alone. Amen.

Now take the piece of paper, ask the Lord to show you the extent of your sin, and write down everything that comes to mind. When you have done this and are content that the list is complete, read through it saying,

I confess my sin of . . . I turn away from it. Lord Jesus, please forgive me and give me the power I need, through your Holy Spirit, never to do it again.

When you have done this with every item on your list, take the piece of paper and burn it. As it burns, read 1 John 1:9, making it personal to yourself—if I confess my sins, he is faithful and just to forgive me my sins and cleanse me from all unrighteousness. Say aloud, 'I am forgiven', and respond to the Lord in whatever way seems appropriate to you at that moment.

Tread Lightly Here

Luke 7:36-50

Tread lightly here—
      For in this place
      a child lost all innocence
      withdrawing to a loneliness
      Only Jesus knows.

Tread lightly here—
      For in this place
      that child found forbidden love
      with deep regret and fear and shame
      Only Jesus knows.

Tread lightly here—
      For in this place
      blood cleansed, created hallowed ground
      and restoration, joy and peace
      Only this child knows.

THE JESUS PRAYER

The Jesus Prayer is the simplest form of Christian prayer because it comprises only one word, *Jesus*. It has been used for many centuries by believers to help them settle into their prayer times. This use of a single word has led some people to suggest that it is making the name of the Lord a kind of mantra. This comes from a misunderstanding, either of Hindu mantras or of the Jesus Prayer. The Hindu mantra is a repeated, rhythmic repetition of a single word or phrase with the aim of emptying the mind. The aim of the Jesus Prayer is to fill the mind with thoughts of God and to connect with him.

Find a place to sit comfortably, place your hands in your lap, and close your eyes. Make a conscious decision to relax. Become aware of your breathing. Starting with your head and face, tense your muscles as you breathe in and relax them as you breathe out. Do the same with your neck and gradually work down the rest of your body. When you have done that, continue to sit quietly for a few moments.

After a minute or so, slow your breathing slightly. Then, as you breathe out, gently and slowly whisper the name, 'Jesus'. Do this five or six times, and then begin to whisper something praiseworthy about him—you are the Prince of Peace. You are the living Word. You are compassionate and gentle. If you run out of ideas, go back to quietly repeating his name. You will soon find yourself experiencing a sense of stillness and quietness before God.

This short and simple prayer can be used on its own or as a way to settle you into your longer devotional time.

A MEDITATION

One of the long established methods of prayer is to actively meditate on a passage of scripture by reading it and placing yourself in the scene. The Gospel narratives are excellent sources for this because they are graphic accounts of people's encounters with Jesus. Here is an example, which uses the story of Jesus healing Bartimaeus from blindness in Mark 10:46-52.

First read the passage through carefully so that you are familiar with it. Then settle yourself and relax, perhaps using the Jesus prayer above. Now imagine you are part of the large crowd following Jesus out of Jericho. Perhaps you have been enthralled by his teaching and are hoping to catch some more of his words before he finally leaves the region. You know Bartimaeus will be by the roadside because he's always there begging. Perhaps you feel a little embarrassed in case he makes a scene in front of this prestigious teacher, impertinently asking for money, taking advantage of the situation.

And then it happens. He doesn't just call out; he shouts. Even worse, he calls Jesus, 'Son of David', Messiah. People nearby are telling him to shut up, be quiet. You're trying to hear what Jesus is saying to his disciples, but you're feeling frustrated because his voice is being drowned out by Bartimaeus and the people around him. Perhaps you join in with the complaints—we all get irritated by circumstances which prevent us from hearing what Jesus is saying.

Bartimaeus calls out repeatedly, 'Jesus, Son of David, have mercy on me!' You don't hear Jesus speak, but suddenly the crowd is quiet except for a few excited voices saying, 'Come on, get up, he wants to talk to you.' Do you feel excited for Bartimaeus, or do you feel jealous that someone like him, the dregs of humanity, is getting the attention of Jesus? Suddenly Bartimaeus is on his feet, someone is taking him by the arm, and the crowd separates to allow them through.

Then Jesus speaks. You hear him ask what Bartimaeus wants him to do. What will he say? Will he ask for money? But Bartimaeus says he wants to see. He wants Jesus to heal his blindness. What's your reaction? Do you think, 'Don't be ridiculous?' Or are you eager to see if Jesus will do one of the miracles you've heard he's done in other towns? Either way, you push through the crowd to see Jesus as he turns to Bartimaeus and says, 'Go, your faith has healed you.' There's no doubt from his reaction that Bartimaeus can now see. He's jumping up and down and praising God. Men are clapping him on the back, women are crying with joy, Jesus is smiling.

Then, Jesus turns to you, still smiling. He looks straight into your eyes, and you feel as though there is no one else in the world besides you and him. He speaks quietly and gently, 'And what about you? What do you want me to do for you?'

Now make your own personal response to Jesus and rest in his presence.

THE BEATITUDES

*R*ead the beatitudes below, one at a time. Reflect for a minute or so on each one. Then respond with the words which follow it before moving on to the next one.

Blessed are the poor in spirit,

for theirs is the kingdom of heaven.

Lord Jesus, I am nothing without you—I am spiritually poor and weak.

Please grant to me all the grace of the kingdom of heaven.

Blessed are those who mourn,

for they will be comforted.

Lord Jesus, cause me to mourn over my sin and my unfaithfulness to you.

Please comfort me with your sweet forgiveness.

Blessed are the meek,

for they will inherit the earth.

Lord Jesus, I do not follow your example of meekness and humility.

Please teach me to walk quietly in your footsteps.

Blessed are those who hunger and thirst for righteousness,

for they will be filled.

Lord Jesus, I am not passionate about righteousness.

Please stir up in me a holy zeal.

Blessed are the merciful,

for they will be shown mercy.

Lord Jesus, you have been so merciful to me.

Please give me the desire to show mercy to others.

Blessed are the pure in heart,

for they will see God.

Lord Jesus, there is a great deal of impurity in my heart.

Please open my eyes to understand what holiness is.

Blessed are the peacemakers,

for they will be called children of God.

Lord Jesus, you are my peace.

Please help me to come to you as a little child.

Blessed are those who are persecuted because of righteousness,

for theirs is the kingdom of heaven.

Lord Jesus, I don't want to be persecuted.

Please help me to stand firm for you to the end.

SAMPLE QUIET TIME

*Y*ou will need:

Your Bible

Your notebook and pen

The Instructions for *The Jesus Prayer* above

The list of statements about the nature and character of God from the
Exercise in the chapter *What Is Worship?*

A short list of who you wish to pray for today

Use *The Jesus Prayer* to settle yourself for your quiet time. Take as long as
you need to feel calm, relaxed, and still.

Allow this to flow into worship. If you find yourself struggling to know what
to say, prompt yourself from your prepared list of statements about God.

When you are ready to move on, ask the Holy Spirit to show you if there is
any sin you need to deal with and respond to his promptings. Remember that
if we confess our sins, he is faithful and just and will forgive us our sins and
purify us from all unrighteousness (1 John 1:9).

Thank him for his forgiveness. Reflect on the previous day and be thankful
for what God has done for you in the past twenty-four hours, especially for any
answered prayer.

Take the list of people you want to pray for. Ask the Lord to guide you into how to pray for each person and situation and then pray what is in your heart. Thank him that he can be trusted to act in each situation for his glory.

Turn to your Bible and ask God to speak to you and teach you from his Word. Read Romans 12:9-21 so that you get a general overview of the passage:

> Love must be sincere. Hate what is evil; cling to what is good. Be devoted to one another in love. Honour one another above yourselves. Never be lacking in zeal, but keep your spiritual fervour, serving the Lord. Be joyful in hope, patient in affliction, faithful in prayer. Share with the Lord's people who are in need. Practise hospitality.
>
> Bless those who persecute you; bless and do not curse. Rejoice with those who rejoice; mourn with those who mourn. Live in harmony with one another. Do not be proud, but be willing to associate with people of low position. Do not be conceited.
>
> Do not repay anyone evil for evil. Be careful to do what is right in the eyes of everyone. If it is possible, as far as it depends on you, live at peace with everyone. Do not take revenge, my dear friends, but leave room for God's wrath, for it is written: 'It is mine to avenge; I will repay,' says the Lord. On the contrary: 'If your enemy is hungry, feed him; if he is thirsty, give him something to drink. In doing this, you will heap burning coals on his head.'
>
> Do not be overcome by evil, but overcome evil with good.

Go back to the beginning of the passage and start to read again. Consider each phrase as you read it asking yourself if God has something to say to you personally through each one—do I love sincerely, do I hate evil, and so on. If a particular phrase grips you, stop and think about it more carefully.

As you read and think, make written notes about what God may be saying to you. Is he convicting you about something you need to change in your life?

Is he revealing something about his character? Is he asking you to do something for another person? Is he giving you insight into how to pray for a certain person or situation?

When you feel God has spoken to you in some way, stop reading. This particular passage is bursting with spiritual nutrition, and you may need to spend several days digesting the whole thing.

Turn your thinking and your notes to prayer. Thank God for speaking to you and respond appropriately to what you have heard. You may need to ask for strength to do his will or to repent of an attitude. You may be prompted to further worship or thanksgiving.

When you feel as though you've done, take a few minutes to simply be still and rest in his presence. Ask him to help you with all that is to come in the rest of the day.

Remember, this is just a sample quiet time. You may want to swap things around, add some singing, listen to a teaching CD, or read a devotional book. You are meeting with the Lover of your soul, and you should do whatever causes you to delight in each other.

GOD REVEALED IN CREATION

For since the creation of the world God's invisible qualities—His eternal power and divine nature—have been clearly seen, being understood from what has been made, so that people are without excuse.

(Rom. 1:20)

God uses the natural world to reveal something about himself to human beings. Perhaps this becomes most clear to us when we are awestruck by the power of a storm at sea or the beauty of a starlit night. These *big* things thunder on the doors of our souls and require us, those who are Christians at least, to take note that our Lord is majestic and powerful. But God also reveals himself in the detail and intricacy of creation. The fact that every human being is different (even identical twins don't share the same fingerprints) shows us that he loves variety and difference. There is great value in taking a part of God's creation—a flower, a stone, an insect—and asking God to speak to you through it.

Perhaps we see the epitome of discovering God in creation in the life of George Washington Carver. He was born a slave in Missouri in around 1864. Despite this start in life, he managed to work his way to a master's degree from Iowa State Agricultural College. He became a research scientist describing his lab as *God's Little Workshop*. Carver discovered that growing peanuts was good for poor quality soil, but no one wanted to cultivate them as there was no market for the resulting produce. So Carver asked God to show him the secrets of the peanut. God answered his prayer by allowing him to discover 300 products, which could be developed from this little bean (botanically speaking it is not a nut). Consequently, by 1940, peanuts had become the second largest crop in the southern United States.

Carver's story is remarkable of course, which is why you will find it all over the Internet. But it is equally remarkable that God can use any part of his creation to speak to us, ordinary people.

Go and find a small piece of God's creation—a flower, a leaf, a stone, a lump of wood, a seed, some fruit. Hold it in your hand and ask the Lord to reveal to you something about his nature from the piece of creation you are holding. Take time to turn it over in your hands, feel its weight and texture, look at its colour and design, think about its purpose. Turn any consequent thoughts about the nature of God to worship and thank him for his creativity.

LOVE DIVINE

I pray that you, being rooted and established in love, may have power, together with all the Lord's holy people, to grasp how wide and long and high and deep is the love of Christ, and to know this love that surpasses knowledge—that you may be filled to the measure of all the fullness of God.

(Eph. 3:17-19)

*T*he Bible is very clear—God's people can know, experientially, that God loves them. Paul doesn't say, 'and to know *about* this love that surpasses knowledge'. It is relatively easy to have an understanding that God loves us; after all he gave us his Son to buy us back so that we can be a part of the Bride of Christ. The Apostle John tells us that God is not simply the God who loves, but the God who is love (1 John 4:8, 16). He cannot refrain from loving us. But there is a huge gulf between believing that God loves me and knowing or experiencing that love.

Paul, in writing to the Ephesians and praying that they would know the love of God which goes beyond knowledge, implies two things. The first is that not all believers have experienced the love of God for themselves. This matches with what I see in the church and my own personal experience. I vividly remember seeing one elderly gentleman, a retired Pentecostal minister, eyes closed during worship, hands raised, and with an expression of absolute delight on his face. He was clearly experiencing the love of God, and I was a little jealous, being in something of a spiritual wilderness at the time and definitely not experiencing God's love in a way that seemed tangible to me.

The second implication of Paul's prayer is that it is possible for every single Christian to feel the love of God. Years after the event I have just described, I was talking with a friend about some difficulties I was experiencing. She said to me, 'But Jesus still loves you.' I was suddenly very aware that I had a silly grin on my face as I replied, 'I know he does.' There was not a single doubt in my mind that I was completely, deeply, and utterly loved by the Lord Jesus. There was a process between those two events during which I experienced his love in such a genuine and powerful way that it completely transformed my relationship with him. So what made the difference?

The most important thing to say is that *revelation* is vital. Head knowledge only becomes heart knowledge when our spiritual eyes are opened, and the only 'Person' who can do that is God. We are dependent on his Holy Spirit. Having said that, there are things we can do to cooperate with him.

Where does this revelation come from? Quite simply, from God's Word. In Colossians, Paul tells us that Jesus is 'the image of the invisible God', (Col. 1:15), which means that Jesus is love incarnate. In other words, to acquire a personal revelation of the love of God, we need to steep ourselves in the Gospels and look for all the evidence we can find of the love that Jesus expressed during his earthly ministry.

Read Luke 8:40-56. In this account, Jesus deals with many different people in different ways. How does he express his love for each individual? Remember that both the woman and the girl would have been regarded as unclean, and that anything or anyone that touched them would become ritually unclean. Is there any aspect of your life which you regard as untouchable, perhaps a sin you've committed or a sin that has been committed against you? You might like to pray the following prayer:

Lord Jesus, I am a damaged and hurting person. I am reluctant to open myself up to you because I am afraid of the shame of being exposed. But I know that I need your loving touch to cleanse and heal me. Please give me the courage to make myself vulnerable to you.

Now rest in his presence and allow him to touch you with his love.

THE GOD WE WORSHIP

*S*ometimes when we pray, we lack faith simply because we forget exactly who it is we're praying to. This short prayer of worship will help you regain your focus.

Lord God, King of creation, you are the one who made everything from nothing. You spoke, and the entire universe came into existence. You made all the galaxies and every individual star with a single command. You made the earth, its plants and animals, from the towering redwoods to the tiniest ant. Your Word says that you see the sparrow fall and that you know the number of hairs on my head. You love humanity so much that you sent your one and only Son to be a sacrifice to pay the debt for sin. And your Word says, 'He who did not spare his own Son, but gave him up for us all—how will he not also, along with him, graciously give us all things?' So I believe you are powerful and loving enough to answer all my prayers. Help me, Lord, to pray with faith, to bring all my concerns to you and to trust that, in your sovereign will, you will include my prayers in your plans. I ask this in the name of Jesus who intercedes for me. Amen.

CAN HE DO IT? YES, HE CAN!

(Luke 5)

*S*ometimes we forget just how able our Saviour is. Reminding ourselves of the variety of his accomplishments recorded in the Gospels can encourage us to believe he will do at least as much in our own lives. Take Luke 5 for example.

Can Jesus, a Carpenter, Teach a Fisherman About Fishing?

One day as Jesus was standing by the lake of Gennesaret, with the people crowding round him and listening to the Word of God, he saw at the water's edge two boats, left there by the fishermen, who were washing their nets. He got into one of the boats, the one belonging to Simon, and asked him to put out a little from shore. Then he sat down and taught the people from the boat. When he had finished speaking, he said to Simon, 'Put out into deep water, and let down the nets for a catch.' Simon answered, 'Master, we've worked hard all night and haven't caught anything. But because you say so, I will let down the nets.' When they had done so, they caught such a large number of fish that their nets began to break. So they signalled to their partners in the other boat to come and help them, and they came and filled both boats so full that they began to sink. When Simon Peter saw this, he fell at Jesus's knees and said, 'Go away from me, Lord. I am a sinful man!' For he and all his companions were astonished at the catch of fish they had taken, and so were James and John, the sons of Zebedee, Simon's partners. Then Jesus said to Simon, 'Don't be afraid. From now on, you will catch men.' So they pulled their boats up on shore, left everything, and followed him.

Yes, He Can!

Can Jesus Touch an Unclean Person Without Being Defiled?

While Jesus was in one of the towns, a man came along who was covered with leprosy. When he saw Jesus, he fell with his face to the ground and begged him, 'Lord, if you are willing, you can make me clean.' Jesus reached out his hand and touched the man. 'I am willing,' he said. 'Be clean!' And immediately, the leprosy left him. Then Jesus ordered him, 'Don't tell anyone, but go, show yourself to the priest and offer the sacrifices that Moses commanded for your cleansing, as a testimony to them.' Yet the news about him spread all the more, so that crowds of people came to hear him and to be healed of their sicknesses. But Jesus often withdrew to lonely places and prayed.

Yes, He Can!

Can Jesus Forgive Sin?

One day as he was teaching, Pharisees and teachers of the law, who had come from every village of Galilee and from Judea and Jerusalem, were sitting there. And the power of the Lord was present for him to heal the sick. Some men came carrying a paralytic on a mat and tried to take him into the house to lay him before Jesus. When they could not find a way to do this because of the crowd, they went up on the roof and lowered him on his mat through the tiles into the middle of the crowd, right in front of Jesus. When Jesus saw their faith, he said, 'Friend, your sins are forgiven.' The Pharisees and the teachers of the law began thinking to themselves, Who is this fellow who speaks blasphemy? Who can forgive sins but God alone? Jesus knew what they were thinking and asked, 'Why are you thinking these things in your hearts? Which is easier: to say, "Your sins are forgiven", or to say, "Get up and walk?"' But that you may know that the Son of Man has authority on earth to forgive sins .... He said to the paralysed man, 'I tell you, get up, take your mat and go home.' Immediately, he stood up in front of them, took what he had been lying on, and went home praising God. Everyone was amazed and gave praise to God. They were filled with awe and said, 'We have seen remarkable things today.'

Yes, He Can!

Can Jesus Be More Attractive Than Wealth?

After this, Jesus went out and saw a tax collector by the name of Levi sitting at his tax booth. 'Follow me,' Jesus said to him, and Levi got up, left everything, and followed him. Then Levi held a great banquet for Jesus at his house, and a large crowd of tax collectors and others were eating with them. But the Pharisees and the teachers of the law who belonged to their sect complained to his disciples, 'Why do you eat and drink with tax collectors and "sinners"?' Jesus answered them, 'It is not the healthy who need a doctor, but the sick. I have not come to call the righteous, but sinners to repentance.'

Yes, He Can!

Can Jesus Transform My Life From Tired Religion to One of Joy?

They said to him, 'John's disciples often fast and pray, and so do the disciples of the Pharisees, but yours go on eating and drinking.' Jesus answered, 'Can you make the guests of the bridegroom fast while he is with them? But the time will come when the bridegroom will be taken from them; in those days they will fast.' He told them this parable: No one tears a patch from a new garment and sews it on an old one. If he does, he will have torn the new garment, and the patch from the new will not match the old. And no one pours new wine into old wineskins. If he does, the new wine will burst the skins, the wine will run out, and the wineskins will be ruined. No, new wine must be poured into new wineskins. And no one after drinking old wine wants the new, for he says, 'The old is better.'

Yes, He Can!

MEDITATING ON FRUITFULNESS

> But the fruit of the Spirit is love, joy, peace, patience, kindness, goodness, faithfulness, gentleness and self-control. Against such things there is no law . . . Since we live by the Spirit, let us keep in step with the Spirit. (Gal. 5:22-25)

The fruit of the Spirit is the evidence of God's work in our lives, and it grows to benefit not only ourselves but, primarily, those around us. Consider each of the nine kinds of fruit and reflect on how that fruit in your life has been used to feed others in the past week. Try to think of a specific example. Then ask the Holy Spirit to grow more of this fruit in you.

When have I been able to demonstrate love to another person?
Holy Spirit, come and bear fruit in me.

When has my joy been used to lift someone else's spirit?
Holy Spirit, come and bear fruit in me.

When has my peace brought calm in a difficult situation?
Holy Spirit, come and bear fruit in me.

When has my patience enabled me to go the extra mile for someone?
Holy Spirit, come and bear fruit in me.

When has my kindness added a blessing to someone else's day?
Holy Spirit, come and bear fruit in me.

When has my goodness set an example to others?
Holy Spirit, come and bear fruit in me.

When has my faithfulness provided a firm foundation for someone else?
Holy Spirit, come and bear fruit in me.

When has my gentleness provided comfort to another person?
Holy Spirit, come and bear fruit in me.

When has my self-control kept me from hurting someone?
Holy Spirit, come and bear fruit in me.

PRAYING A PSALM

I am grateful to Nancy Missler for her research into the worship in Solomon's Temple. In her book *Private Worship: The Key To Joy*, she quotes from Chaim Richman's *A House of Prayer For All Nations* and lists the Psalms used each day as the priests entered the Temple court. These were:

Sunday: Psalm 24
Monday: Psalm 48
Tuesday: Psalm 82
Wednesday: Psalm 94
Thursday: Psalm 81
Friday: Psalm 93
Saturday: Psalm 92

Christians have always loved the Psalms and found them to be helpful in their personal devotions as well as in corporate worship. But sometimes, we forget that they were written as heartfelt prayers and end up reciting them rather than praying them. One way to make these Psalms our own is to rewrite them in our own words. Let's try this with the first of these daily Psalms.

Psalm 24

Of David. A psalm.

(*A song of praise to God by Lynda*)

The earth is the Lord's, and everything in it, the world, and all who live in it;

(*The whole planet belongs to God. So does everything and everyone who lives on it*)

For he founded it upon the seas and established it upon the waters.

(*He built it from the foundations up*)

Who may ascend the hill of the Lord? Who may stand in his holy place?

(*Who can come to such a great God and stand in his presence?*)

He who has clean hands and a pure heart, who does not lift up his soul to an idol or swear by what is false.

(*Only someone who has put themselves right with him and has him as their only God*)

He will receive blessing from the Lord and vindication from God his Saviour.

(*Those who come to the Lord as their Saviour will be blessed and shown to be righteous*)

Such is the generation of those who seek him, who seek your face, O God of Jacob.

(*This will be true of all who seek the face of our God*)

Lift up your heads, O you gates, be lifted up, you ancient doors, that the King of glory may come in.

(*Look up and open the gates of your hearts so that our glorious King may come in*)

Who is this King of glory? The Lord strong and mighty, the Lord mighty in battle.

(*Who is this glorious King? It is the Lord who is so powerful that he wins every battle*)

Lift up your heads, O you gates, lift them up, you ancient doors, that the King of glory may come in.

(Look up and open the gates of your hearts so that our glorious King may come in)
Who is he, this King of glory? The Lord Almighty—he is the King of glory.
(Who is this glorious King? Almighty God—he is the glorious King we welcome)

This isn't intended to be an alternative translation but an expression of the truth of the psalm in our own words. Why not try it yourself with one of the other daily Psalms above.

ANOTHER LOVE LETTER TO JESUS

*B*eloved Lord Jesus,

You are so gracious to me. You keep showing your love to me. You keep speaking gently to my spirit. I love you. I want to be faithful to you. Yet I am so weak. Help me, please. Give me extra strength so I can stay alert to spend quality time with you.

Lord Jesus, I need you. I keep saying it because I keep discovering greater depths of my need. I am nothing without you. Yet you are so loving and compassionate towards me. Jesus, I want to grow ever closer to you in love and obedience. I want to be that living sacrifice, which Paul talks about in Romans 12. I want to give my life to you. But I can't even do that on my own.

Jesus, you inspire adoration in those whose spiritual eyes are open to see you. Thank you for opening my eyes. Thank you for gently touching my heart and revealing the beauty of your perfect love. There is nothing like your love. It is so sweet, so tender. It is utterly delightful.

Lord Jesus, King of kings, Lord of lords, you are absolute perfection. One day, every knee will bow in worship when you reveal yourself to all humanity. Thank you for the privilege of bowing the knee to you now, of worshipping you now, of intimacy with you now. It's not just about the hope of heaven, but the reality of you living in me at this moment. In the words of the Song of Songs, 'I delight to sit in your shade.'

I weep as I think about the wonderful knowledge of your love. Bless you Lord Jesus, bless you, my Master. Your love fills me until I feel I cannot contain it.

I love you back with the love with which you have loved me. As John says, we love because you first loved us. The love I feel for you is simply a giving back of the love you have already bestowed on me. It is too wonderful to comprehend. You do it all; yet you invite me to participate in the greatest love story in the history of the universe. You have made me loveable by loving me. You have made me loving by loving me.

Oh, let the love flow between us and out to others you love.

Amen.

BARBECUING WITH JESUS

'I'm going out to fish,' Simon Peter told them, and they said, 'We'll go with you.' So they went out and got into the boat, but that night they caught nothing. Early in the morning, Jesus stood on the shore, but the disciples did not realise that it was Jesus. He called out to them, 'Friends, haven't you any fish?' 'No,' they answered. He said, 'Throw your net on the right side of the boat and you will find some.' When they did, they were unable to haul the net in because of the large number of fish. Then the disciple whom Jesus loved said to Peter, 'It is the Lord!' As soon as Simon Peter heard him say, 'It is the Lord', he wrapped his outer garment around him (for he had taken it off) and jumped into the water. The other disciples followed in the boat, towing the net full of fish, for they were not far from shore, about a hundred yards. When they landed, they saw a fire of burning coals there with fish on it and some bread. Jesus said to them, 'Bring some of the fish you have just caught.' Simon Peter climbed aboard and dragged the net ashore. It was full of large fish, but even with so many, the net was not torn. Jesus said to them, 'Come and have breakfast.' None of the disciples dared ask him, 'Who are you?' They knew it was the Lord. Jesus came, took the bread, and gave it to them, and did the same with the fish. This was now the third time Jesus appeared to his disciples after he was raised from the dead. When they had finished eating, Jesus said to Simon Peter, 'Simon son of John, do you truly love me more than these?'

'Yes, Lord,' he said, 'you know that I love you.' Jesus said, 'Feed my lambs.' (John 21:3-15)

Good friends go out together for coffee, couples go out for romantic dinners, and Jesus seems to have constantly been eating at parties thrown in his honour. Although he was often physically tired and frequently sought out places to be alone, he never turned away anyone who came to him.

And often he invited people to come to him and spend time with him.

One of those occasions was after the resurrection when the disciples found him on the beach barbecuing fish for breakfast. It is such an ordinary scene, and yet it was the prelude to an extraordinary conversation between Peter and his Lord which transformed him from a broken man to the leader of the church.

Peter could easily have missed out on the extraordinary if he hadn't embraced the ordinary. I wonder if, at any point between sighting Jesus and speaking to him, Peter thought to himself, 'I just can't face him after what I did.'

The wisdom of Jesus is always remarkable. Instead of immediately getting into conversation about Peter's failure, he simply welcomes him into the circle of fellowship, sharing the food together. Like the prodigal son, Peter knows he is accepted by the welcome he is given.

Of course, the difficult conversation still has to take place, but it is a very different one to that which it could have been if Peter was still feeling distanced from Jesus.

When we feel we've let the Lord down in some way, we often find it hard to know how to approach him about it because of our sense of shame. But Jesus is always waiting to welcome us back.

If you are feeling reluctant to face Jesus for some reason, you might like to try this.

Find a place to be alone and bring something to eat and drink. It could be a full-blown picnic or simply a bread roll and a glass of wine. Jesus will be with you because he always is. Be conscious of that fact. Eat and drink in his presence. Then, when you are ready, simply say to him, 'Here I am', and wait for him to speak.

He may put a thought or a passage of scripture into your mind, or you may become aware of him gently touching your spirit. Be willing to hear in whatever way he may choose to speak to you, and if it doesn't happen immediately, trust that he will do so in his own time.

Above all, be assured that he still loves you and still wants to enjoy your company.

An Undivided Heart

*I*n Psalm 86:11, David prays, *give me an undivided heart.* The more we develop our prayer lives and the closer we get to Jesus, the more aware we become that there are so many other things vying for our affections and how vulnerable we are to being drawn away after those inferior loves.

We are often unaware that something or someone has been elevated in our heart above the position we give to Jesus until he puts his finger on the problem—our own heart lies to us. In Jeremiah 17:9, the Lord tells us that *the heart is deceitful above all things and beyond cure.* We cannot make our hearts better. They are afflicted with incurable disease. But notice how David surrenders the state of his heart to God. He knows that divine intervention is needed if he is to become wholehearted towards the Lord.

So what will God do? Will he fix our hearts? No!

No, he has a better plan. See what he says in Ezekiel 11:19:

> I will give them an undivided heart and put a new spirit in them; I will remove from them their heart of stone and give them a heart of flesh.

And again in Ezekiel 36:26:

> I will give you a new heart and put a new spirit in you; I will remove
> from you your heart of stone and give you a heart of flesh.

There are no bypasses or valve replacements here but a whole heart
transplant, a heart whose treasure is Jesus and nothing else (Luke 12:34). Pray
with me:

> Lord God, I know that I am not wholehearted towards you. My heart
> is divided, and I often place other concerns before you. Please forgive
> me for my unfaithfulness. Just as David prayed, I ask that you would
> give me an undivided heart. Your word promises an undivided heart
> and a new spirit. Please take my old heart and give me a heart that
> is wholeheartedly for you. Take away my love of sin, my attitude of
> compromise with the world, and my love of self. Give me instead the
> heart that beats with the love of Jesus for you and for those around
> me. I ask it in his precious name and for his sake so that I may bring
> glory to you. Amen.

THE PRACTICE OF THE PRESENCE OF GOD

*B*rother Lawrence was a French Carmelite monk born in 1614 who served chiefly in the monastery kitchen. The collection of his letters and records of conversations with him have been compiled in a book entitled *The Practice of the Presence of God*. It has been given this name as it is the phrase Brother Lawrence used to describe his personal method of prayer.

His method was simple yet profound—it was to endeavour to constantly turn his heart and towards God and to do everything as for the Lord (Col. 3:23).

> We can do little things for God; I turn the cake that is frying on the
> pan for love of Him, and that done, if there is nothing else to call
> me, I prostrate myself in worship before Him, who has given me
> grace to work; afterwards I rise happier than a king. It is enough
> for me to pick up but a straw from the ground for the love of God.
> (Brother Lawrence)

This is not complicated, but it is difficult. Our minds constantly stray to other thoughts either casually or because the particular task at hand requires concentration. However if we can learn to offer all our activity to him and to practise the presence of God in those moments when our minds are less absorbed, we can begin to still have our hearts set on him at those other times when we are more busy.

Dear Lord Jesus, I thank you for the example of Brother Lawrence. It is my desire that I should live in such a way that all that I do is for your glory, whether it is the mundane parts of my life or the spiritual aspects of it. Help me to do everything as if doing it for you, and help me to keep my heart and mind fixed on you throughout the day. Amen

LOVE ONE ANOTHER

By this all men will know that you are my disciples, if you love one another.

(John 13:35)

*T*he twelve disciples were what my Dad would call a *motley crew*. I doubt they would ever have gathered themselves together if Jesus hadn't called each of them to himself. There were small businessmen and tax collectors, never a good combination in any age. There was a freedom fighter and a collaborator for that's basically what zealots and tax collectors were. There was the extrovert Peter and the contemplative John. They were full of rivalry:

> They came to Capernaum. When he was in the house, he asked them, What were you arguing about on the road? But they kept quiet because on the way they had argued about who was the greatest. Sitting down, Jesus called the Twelve and said, If anyone wants to be first, he must be the very last, and the servant of all. He took a little child and had him stand among them. Taking him in his arms, he said to them, Whoever welcomes one of these little children in my name welcomes me; and whoever welcomes me does not welcome me but the one who sent me.

> Teacher, said John, we saw a man driving out demons in your
> name and we told him to stop, because he was not one of us. Do not
> stop him, Jesus said. No-one who does a miracle in my name can
> in the next moment say anything bad about me, for whoever is not
> against us is for us. (Mark 9:33-40)

So it is perhaps hardly surprising that one of the final things Jesus instructs them is to love one another. I am prepared to hazard a guess that there is no church that doesn't still need to hear and respond to those words of Jesus.

Here is an exercise, which I have used several times in the past in small groups to encourage people to look upon one another with an increasingly loving attitude, but it works just as well individually.

Think about a small group of Christians of which you are a part—a home group, Bible study group, prayer group, or similar. Try to think of a group which has between five and fifteen members. Any smaller and the exercise won't mean much, any larger, and it will just take too long.

Take a piece of paper, and write everyone's name on it. Then next to each name, write something about that person which you appreciate and can thank God for. If you are someone like me, there will be some people you could fill a whole page for and others where you're really scratching your head just to think of one thing. Discipline yourself, and write just one thing for each person, and if you're really struggling, pray for help. If you're doing this in private, you could even resort to, *I thank you that you are using this person to teach me patience.*

Then pray a prayer of thanksgiving for each person and ask the Lord to help you love them more.

If you were to do this exercise in a small group, you could have a piece of paper for each person with their name at the bottom, and then pass it round so that everyone can write their comments, folding the top down each time so that the comments remain private. The sheets can then be returned to the person whose name can still be seen at the bottom so they can read the appreciative thoughts of their brothers and sisters in the group. It is a tremendous way to show love and to encourage one another.

SHOW ME YOUR HEART

We do not know what we ought to pray for, but the Spirit himself
intercedes for us with groans that words cannot express.

(Rom. 8:26)

*T*his follows on quite naturally from the previous devotion, but it
comes with a health warning attached—it *will* change you.

There have been times when I have struggled to know how to pray for someone. It may be that it is a person I don't particularly like, or it may be someone I
care deeply about but have run out of ideas for how to pray for them. On some
such occasions, I have prayed, *Lord, please show me your heart for this person.*

The results have been quite overwhelming at times as the Spirit answers
and pours in knowledge of something of the feelings of love he has towards this
person. It is always slightly different, but it is always loving, and it is mingled
with the joy, compassion, and concern that he feels. I know that what he reveals
is just a tiny part of what is in *his* heart because the *human* heart is incapable of
containing a fraction of it. Also, he never shows me any specific details about
what is going on in that person's life—that is none of my business. But what he
does share of his heart equips me to pray passionately for the person, perhaps
with those groans that words cannot express, usually with tears. It is also very
humbling as I realise just how great and powerful his love for individual people

is. We can say, very tritely sometimes, *Jesus loves you.* Those words can never do justice to the power of his emotions.

It can be completely spiritually draining to receive such a revelation from God, so it is not something I do with any great consistency. But I would commend this practice to you for occasional use to help you in your intercession for others during your devotional times.

APART FROM ME

I am the true vine, and my Father is the gardener. He cuts off every
branch in me that bears no fruit, while every branch that does
bear fruit he prunes so that it will be even more fruitful. You are
already clean because of the word I have spoken to you. Remain
in me, and I will remain in you. No branch can bear fruit by itself;
it must remain in the vine. Neither can you bear fruit unless you
remain in me. I am the vine; you are the branches. If a man remains
in me and I in him, he will bear much fruit; apart from me you can
do nothing.

(John 15:1-5)

*T*his is one of those well-known passages, which we tend to skim
through because it is so familiar. But let me draw your attention to a few little
insights.

Firstly, those two little words *clean* and *prune* are actually the same word
katharos from which we get our English word *cathartic*. It is the same word
which appears in John 13:10 where Jesus says to Peter,

A person who has had a bath needs only to wash his feet; his whole
body is clean. And you are clean, though not every one of you.

This word *katharos* literally means *pure, guiltless, ceremonially clean, free from sin*. Look again at the first passage. We are clean because of the words the Lord Jesus has spoken to us. What are those words? They are the words of eternal life (John 6:68).

Secondly, see how dependent we are on the Lord Jesus, *apart from me you can do nothing*. We are not simply dependent on him for our salvation, but for everything. Once we were part of another vine and received our strength from its sap. But now we have been grafted into the true vine, and our only source of strength is Jesus. Sadly, we do not always recognise this and try to go on in our old strength.

But unless we remain in Jesus, and he in us, we will be unable to bear any fruit; we will be able to do nothing.

Devoted to Prayer

Devote yourselves to prayer, being watchful and thankful.

(Col. 4:2)

I imagine that the church at Colossae avidly pored over the words of Paul's letter, eager to get to grips with all he had to say to them, especially when it had opened with such encouraging and inspiring words. Here, at the heart of what he is telling them about how to live the Christian life, we see how fundamental prayer is.

Let's think for a moment about what that word *devote* means.

The Cambridge online dictionary (dictionary.cambridge.org) gives the following definition,

> *to give all of something, especially your time, effort or love, or yourself, to something you believe in or to a person.* (author's emphasis)

According to oxforddictionaries.com, its origin is from a Latin word meaning to *consecrate* or to *vow*.

In the Old Testament, something which was devoted to God was given completely to him and could not be reclaimed or redeemed. This was done by either handing the item over to the priests or completely destroying it. Remember how Hannah, desperate for a child, prayed.

> And she made a vow, saying, O Lord Almighty, if you will only look upon your servant's misery and remember me, and not forget your servant but give her a son, then I will give him to the Lord for all the days of his life, and no razor will ever be used on his head. (1 Sam. 1:11)

The mention of the razor is significant because one of the signs that a person was devoted to God was that their hair was never cut (see Numbers 6, Judges 13).

So it seems that to be devoted to prayer means to give all of yourself to prayer, to be totally committed to it.

Ask yourself what that might mean for you in terms of time, energy, and passion.

ARE YOU WILLING?

If you are willing and obedient, you will eat the good things of the land.

But if you refuse and rebel, you will be devoured by the sword.

(Isa. 1:19-20)

When I ask for help from my children, there are two possible reactions. The first is that they respond enthusiastically and can't wait to get on with what I've asked of them. The second and far more common reaction is a reluctance so powerful that it requires something akin to dynamite to get them moving.

We can behave like this with God. We read his Word and we discover that there is some way in which we fail to live up to his standard. Gossiping might be an example. Now the willing child, discovering her heavenly Father does not want her to gossip, will make every effort to conform to his will. But the rebellious child will find all sorts of excuses for not complying; after all, it isn't really gossip if I'm sharing the information for prayer, is it?

The willing child is teachable. He listens to sermons with the expectation that God will speak directly to his heart about his own life. The rebellious child will challenge even the words of scripture. I remember a conversation with one person in which I referred to Romans 8:1 saying *there is no condemnation for those who are in Christ* to which this person replied, 'There is when it comes to . . . We stand on very dangerous ground when we set ourselves against the direct teaching of Scripture.'

The willing child doesn't wait to be asked but looks for opportunities to do the right thing. The rebellious child will not even do what is asked of them. Romans 12:1 tells us to offer ourselves as a living sacrifice. It's not a popular concept these days, this idea of willing sacrifice. You can go into any Christian bookshop and see titles such as *7 Steps For Answered Prayer*, or *How To Be A Happy Christian*, or even *The Financial Benefits Of Tithing*. But where are the books about living sacrificially for Jesus, where is the one called *Ultimate Obedience*? We forget that we are not our own; we were bought with a price and a very dear one indeed (1 Cor. 6:19-20).

The Word of God through Isaiah offers blessings for willingness and obedience and severe consequences for rebellion. The question is, how willing are you? Are you prepared to be obedient to the call to live sacrificially for Jesus, or are you placing limits on what you're willing to give?

In an attitude of prayer, ask the Lord to show you if there are any areas of your life that you are unwilling to sacrifice to him. Is your time your own, or does it belong to Jesus? What about your material resources, your money? Are you fully committed to your brothers and sisters in Christ, or will you look the other way when they're in need? Is there any aspect where you say, thus far and no further? Wrestle with these things until they are submitted to Jesus.

BE SILENT

Be silent before the Lord and wait expectantly for Him.

(Ps. 37:7)

*A*t our home group, once we were asked to read Psalm 37 and pick out verses, which we felt spoke to us as individuals. This was the verse I chose, but I was surprised by the almost universal comments that being silent before God was something people found difficult.

Being silent before God is not an optional extra in our prayer lives. We are instructed several times in scripture to do this, to *be still and know that I am God* (Ps. 46:10).

For many of us, it is not something which comes naturally. It is a skill, which has to be learnt through practice. It takes time, which we all know is at a premium. But most of us do have the time to devote to this. If we choose:

We can turn off the TV for an hour;

We can go to bed earlier and get up earlier;

We can use our lunch break.

We find time for the things we really want to do. We can find time to learn to be still before God.

We should be willing to be still before God simply because it is what he asks of us. But there are benefits to us.

Firstly, we get to know the Lord in a more deeply personal way. People falling in love tend to spend an inordinate amount of time gazing into one another's eyes. They do not consider this as wasted time. It is part of the bonding process. In the same way, being still and gazing upon the Lord brings us closer to him.

Secondly, we learn the sound of his voice as he whispers into our spirit. His is a still, small voice (1 Kng. 19:12), and we cannot hope to hear it if our own voice is clamouring in our ears all the time. One of the mistakes people make in seeking guidance is that they look for signs (fine in so far as it goes—Matt. 12:39) but neglect to listen to the voice of God.

Thirdly, it is the most refreshing and restorative experience we can have. Being still before God allows him to touch and heal the hurting places in our hearts and minds. When we are still before him and he *unveils himself,* to quote from Andrew Murray, we see him as he is—Almighty God, Lord of creation, the One against whom no one can stand—and ourselves as we are, his beloved children. All the stresses and strains of our lives are put into perspective as we recognise his authority in our lives.

So why not take a few moments every day this week to be still, fix your eyes on Jesus, and tell him you love him?

WALKING THE WALK

I know the plans I have for you.

(Jer. 25:9)

*T*his well-known verse is often quoted as comfort for people going through difficult times. My reaction has sometimes been, 'Well, I wish he would tell me.'

It's easy to trot out this passage and others like it when someone else is in the midst of confusion. 'All things work together for good,' we say to the friend who has had the proverbial rug pulled from under their feet.

All sorts of things crowd our minds when we face adversity—what should I do, why doesn't God do something, where did I go wrong? We think we've missed God's will somewhere along the line, and our current experiences are the result of that.

Sometimes the fear of making a mistake, of stepping outside of the will of God, and attracting the wrath of God causes us to become so paralysed we don't do anything. We believe the corollary of the words of Job's friends, that if we make a mistake, God will punish us severely.

So we don't step out in faith to try new things for God. We lay out *fleeces* (Judg. 6:36-40), and we wait for confirmations from outside sources.

It is true that our God is a jealous God who can be angry. But his anger is not with those trying to serve him out of genuine love for him. His anger is against those who set up idols in their lives or hearts and turn away from loving and worshipping him. God spoke through the prophet Isaiah in Isaiah 30:21 to say the following,

> If you turn to the right or to the left, you will hear a voice behind
> you saying, 'this is the way, walk in it.

The message is clear. If you want to know the direction you should take, then you have to be moving, trusting the Lord to speak up if you're headed in the wrong direction.

We forget that God is far less concerned about whether we're in the right place geographically than he is in the state of our hearts.

> This is what the Lord requires of you, to act justly, to love mercy and
> to walk humbly with your God. (Mic. 6:8)

Everything else is a side issue. The things we think are important to get right—which church we're in, what our ministry is to be, whether we are called to work with a particular group—all these things are meaningless if we are not walking humbly with our God.

I heard a missionary to Bhutan talk about the awesome beauty of her adopted homeland. 'But,' she said, 'it doesn't appear beautiful if your heart is not right with God.'

When you pray for yourself, are you seeking details of guidance, or is your desire to have God work on your motives and your heart's attitude to him? When you pray for others, do you ask for their problems to be solved, questions answered, or do you pray that they will grow to become more like Jesus, walking humbly with God?

BIBLIOGRAPHY

A Short and Easy Method of Prayer. Guyon, Jeanne. Cosimo Inc. 92 pp

Breaking Through in Prayer. Chesney, D. Marshall Pickering. 96 pp

Death of a Guru. Maharaj, R. Hodder & Stoughton. 208 pp

Discipleship. Watson, D. Hodder & Stoughton. 287 pp

God's Chosen Fast. Wallis, A. Christian Literature Crusade.

How to Pray. Torrey, RA. Moody Press. 128 pp

Life of the Beloved. Nouwen, H. Crossroad. 160 pp

Listening to God. Huggett, Joyce. Hodder & Stoughton (15 Aug 2005). 240 pp

Personality and Prayer. Fowke, Ruth. CWR. 96 pp

Prayer. Bunyan, John. *Banner of Truth.* 172 pp

Prayer. Spurgeon, Charles. Whitaker House. 190 pp

Prayers of Life. Quoist, Michel. Gill & Macmillan. 135 pp

Prevailing Prayer. Moody, DL. Ambassador. 121 pp

Private Worship: The Key to Joy. Missler, Nancy. Kings High Way. 194 pp

Revelations of Divine Love. Julian of Norwich. Penguin Classics. 240 pp

Revival Praying. Ravenhill, Leonard. Bethany House. 176 pp

Rees Howells Intercessor. Grubb, Norman. Lutterworth Press. 292 pp

Search the Scriptures. Stibbs, Alan. IVP. 541 pp

Seeing and Savoring Jesus Christ. Piper, John. IVP 128 pp

The Essentials of Prayer. Bounds, EM. Kindle

The Grace Outpouring. Godwin, R. David C Cook, 192 pp

The Hour That Changes the World. Eastman, Dick. Chosen Books. 160 pp

The Joy of Answered Prayer. Moody, DL. Whitaker House. 154 pp

The Power of Simple Prayer. Meyer, Joyce. Hodder & Stoughton. 320 pp

The Practice of the Presence of God. Brother Lawrence. Wilder Publications. 104 pp

The Prayer Life. Murray, Andrew. Diggory Press. 108 pp

The Pursuit of God. Tozer, AW. Authentic Lifestyle.

The True Vine. Murray, Andrew. Moody Classics.

Too Busy Not to Pray. Hybels, Bill. IVP. 192 pp

When I Don't Desire God. Piper, John. IVP. 272 pp

Lightning Source UK Ltd.
Milton Keynes UK
UKOW04f0619130913

217124UK00002B/166/P